The Magic of Miniatures

Compiled and written by

JO CLAY

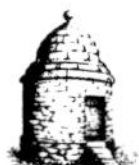

1991

Mendip Publishing

Castle Cary Press, Somerset

Illustrations on the Cover

Front cover: DAME PEGGY ASHCROFT **3″ × 2½″ (76 × 64 mm)**
by Pauline Denyer SLm Des.RCA HS

WINTER FLOWERS **3½″ × 3″ (89 × 76 mm)**
by Margaret Ryder VPRMS SWA FSBA HS SM

TREASURE **3⅛″ × 2½″ (80 × 64 mm)**
by Henry Saxon RMS HS

Back cover: JULIA FOWLER **(watercolour on ivory) 3¾″ × 3″ (95 × 76 mm)**
by W. P. Mundy RMS HS FSCD

SEEDS AND LEAVES AND TINY TOADSTOOLS
(watercolour on 40 year-old ivory) 3″ × 4″ (76 × 100 mm)
by Suzanne Lucas FLS FPRMS FPSBA SWA Hon.HS

COMMON BLUE AT LANGTON MATRAVERS **3″ × 2⅛″ (76 × 54 mm)**
by Meg Kingston HS

ICEBERG ROSE AND STRAWBERRIES **3″ × 4″ (76 × 100 mm)**
by Sheila Fairman RMS FSBA SWA HS

HYDRANGEAS **(oil on board) 3⅞″ × 2⅞″ (100 × 72 mm)**
by Robert Hughes RMS HS

EVENING LIGHT **3⅗″ × 2½″ (92 × 64 mm)**
by Rosalind Pierson RMS HS (Founder) MMAS

Photography by: DAVID TITCHENER, A.B.I.P., A.M.P.A.

Some transparencies lent by the artists or owners of the miniatures or galleries duly acknowledged where possible.

ISBN 0-905903-29-3

Printed at Castle Cary Press
Mendip Publishing
Castle Cary
Somerset BA7 7AN

The Magic of Miniatures

JO CLAY

This book is dedicated to all Creative People
who make the world a better place.

Limning . . . is a thing apart from
all other painting or drawing . . .
and it excelleth all other painting
whatsoever in sundry points.

NICHOLAS HILLIARD (c. 1600)

A BOOK TO INTRODUCE THE ART OF MINIATURE PAINTING

TO THOSE NOT ACQUAINTED WITH THE WONDER IT PROVIDES

and

FOR THOSE WHO HOPE TO LEARN MORE ABOUT THE

TECHNIQUE FROM THOSE WELL-QUALIFIED TO GIVE IT

Thirty-two of the finest miniature painters in Britain today, who represent many more, have generously given their time, as well as providing information about their expertise and allowing us to have a record of their miniature paintings in colour.

CONTENTS

Abbreviations

A list of abbreviations and their meanings are given below:

ARMS	Associate Member, Royal Society of Miniature Painters, Sculptors and Gravers
FLS	Fellow of the Linnean Society
FRSA	Fellow of the Royal Society of Arts
FSIAD	Fellow of the Society of Industrial Artists and Designers
HS	Hilliard Society (Exhibiting Artist Member)
MAA	Miniature Artists of America Society
MASF	Miniature Arts Society of Florida
MASNJ	Miniature Arts Society of New Jersey
MMAS	Montana Miniature Arts Society
MPSG	Miniature Painters, Sculptors and Gravers - Washington DC
MSIAD	Member of the Society of Industrial Artists and Designers
NDD	National Design Diploma
PMC	Member of the British Print Makers' Council
PS	Pastel Society
RI	Royal Institute of Painters in Watercolours
RMS	Member of the Royal Society of Miniature Painters, Sculptors and Gravers
SBA	Society of Botanical Artists
SLm	Society of Limners
SM	Society of Miniaturists
SWA	Society of Women Artists
USM	Ulster Society of Miniaturists
USWA	Ulster Society of Watercolour Artists

ACKNOWLEDGEMENTS

My unbounded gratitude goes to all the Miniature Painters featured in this book, without whose help it would not have been written. Also, for the generous loan of valuable miniatures which David Titchener, ABIP, AMPA, photographed for the reproductions, taking a great deal of trouble on our behalf.

I am very grateful, too, to the private owners of some of the miniatures who were kind enough to lend them; and to the miniaturists who made their own transparencies available. Mrs Katherine Parkinson and Jillian Llewellyn Lloyd of the Llewellyn Alexander Gallery have been most helpful with advice and the loan of transparencies from their own collection, including the work of Pamela Davis, Elaine Fellows and Eric Morton.

I have many people, too, to thank for especial generosity in making this book possible, amongst whom are Sheila Fairman, Jennifer Buxton, Robert Hughes and Mrs Phoebe Sholto Douglas, who had the confidence to support me from the beginning. Also John Hamilton for his generosity. I have also to thank Elizabeth Davys Wood, PSLm SWA for first nurturing my interest in miniature painting, as she has done for other artists. Elaine Fellows has been most thoughtful in alerting the Rover Company to the need for financial help in launching this book, and for their welcome response. My gratitude goes to Sydney Shorthouse for advice, and teaching me how to photograph miniature paintings.

I have to thank Heather O. Catchpole who has given much practical help and advice, and W. P. Mundy for a great deal of information about the various techniques. Phoebe Sholto Douglas most generously allowed me access to her six-part 'History of Miniature Painting', first published in *The Artist*. Also to Irene Briers, Editor of the *Leisure Painter* for promising assistance with advertising and a book review, as well as providing me with back copies of the magazine for features by Margaret Ryder, Sheila Fairman, Pamela Davis and W. P. Mundy. Philip Berrill, the 'Flying Artist', has offered to send information to his clientele about 'The Magic of Miniatures'. Maureen Pearson, Margaret Ryder and Barbara Valentine have written cheerful, encouraging letters to help overcome some of the problems that occasionally made the task difficult. Thanks go, too, to Pam Morgan for practical help. Most of all I have to thank the members of the newly-founded Sherborne Miniature Painting Society, whose President is Sheila Sanford, RI, RMS, for the members' continued support through the many months of hard work involved with its production; and to Peter Stone, in the Little Art Shop,

Sherborne, for his interest and searching for me through catalogues for addresses or information.

Roy Sanford has given invaluable advice and assistance with the front cover. I am particularly glad about the pleasure Dame Peggy Ashcroft is providing for everyone by having accepted personally the invitation to be featured in the miniature portrait on the cover by Pauline Denyer, which was exhibited in the RMS Exhibition in 1990.

Finally, credit goes to Mrs Sue Burton, co-founder of the Hilliard Society, for asking me to do the 'Biographies' for the Society Newsletters; without them this book would not have been written. Most of all I have to thank my husband, Anthony, whose interest during the slow, progressive stages of preparation of this book, and his patience and help with the proof-reading, have been invaluable.

JO CLAY
June 1991

PREFACE

For anyone wishing to learn the rudiments of miniature painting, the availability of suitable books or tutors is limited. Many artists have taught themselves after attending one of the London exhibitions of the Royal Society of Miniature Painters, Sculptors and Gravers (referred to throughout, for brevity, as the RMS), where some of the best miniature paintings in the world can be seen. Close observation of them, followed by individual trial and error, has enabled some artists to teach themselves to obtain the intricate detail of a miniature painting and the requisite degree of perfection with its characteristic luminous quality. This is achieved by applying many thin layers of watercolour, oil or acrylic paint, known as 'glazing'.

Most of the miniaturists in this book advise a close study of the miniature paintings in the Victoria and Albert Museum, in South Kensington. Another way is to visit some stately homes or National Trust great houses, where miniatures from the 17th or 18th century may be amongst their family heirlooms. Alternatively, joining one of the miniature painting societies (listed at the back of the book), is also most helpful. It provides the opportunity for competent miniaturists to exhibit their work in a gallery with other miniature painters.

Sadly, the Royal Academy has ceased to have the large section in which they used to have miniatures on display in their Summer Exhibitions. Miniature painting is a very demanding and beautiful art form, and many people would like to see the return of the miniatures to that great Gallery, which allows so few now.

However, more and more galleries and exhibitions are accepting miniature paintings, just as the number of enthusiasts and artists tempted into painting them is increasing. This book is designed to appeal also to the 'new' miniaturists and artists who appreciate the fine details in paintings. The book has been written for them with the most generous help of many professional miniaturists. Every one is a Member or Associate Member of the RMS, or is exhibiting work with the RMS or the Hilliard Society, with the exception of Michael Pierce, Professional Profilist and Silhouettist, who is widely known in this country and internationally.

The author would like to have included many more of the many fine miniaturists, in the various societies, but it was not practical, so a representative few had to be chosen. Three relative newcomers, who have shown their work with the Hilliard Society and RMS, are also represented, so that their work may be compared with the long-standing professional miniaturists.

The range of subjects in miniature paintings or drawings may be painted on a variety of different surfaces, though watercolour tends to be the most common medium. The others are oils, acrylic or pencils, sometimes even pastel, and the surface may be on various types of smooth paper such as Arches Hot Pressed Paper or ivorine (a substitute for ivory), card, plaster, a smooth card-like material called Ivorex or ivory (when obtainable). The ivory miniaturists are using now is likely to be at least forty years old, and would not qualify for criticism from conservationists.

Normally, artists hoping to show their miniatures in the RMS Exhibition, held annually in November, submit five of their miniatures. Full Members may send in seven. If five are accepted, those hoping to become associate members (ARMS) may apply the following year and thereafter to become ARMS and can continue to do so until it is achieved. There are a number of rules stipulated, referring to the size of the paintings permitted. Good presentation is essential.

Each miniaturist in this book usually specializes in one or two subjects, but the artists have been listed in alphabetical order to avoid being categorized under particular subjects which may not be an accurate description of their range of work.

Finally, it is intriguing to contemplate the part that *Magic* and *Chance* play in our lives. The book has been given its title because of chance meetings or occurrences contributing to its creation. Also because it seems magical that so much professionalism has been gathered together to present a happy and magical offering that it seems is much needed in our lives today. Holding a miniature in the palm of one's hand or examining it minutely under a magnifying glass, reveals the luminosity, vibrancy and colours as in fairies' wings. It is hoped many more people will be aware of this magic, rather like the children in Barrie's *Peter Pan* who learned to fly. It is the unbelievability of achieving something they never imagined possible, that many people discover through the study of miniature painting.

If this book introduces its readers to a new and fascinating hobby, it will be worthwhile. Collectors may be encouraged to visit the miniature exhibitions advertised in *The Artist* or the *Leisure Painter* magazines. But whether these 'jewels' hang on a wall, stand on a mantlepiece or sideboard, or are worn personally in pendants or brooches, miniatures give people great happiness. That is magical.

ABOUT MINIATURE PAINTING and its ORIGINS

It is worth defining what is meant by a 'miniature painting' before taking a look at its background in Britain from the 16th century onwards. None of it encompasses the miniature painting of Persia, India or Turkey, which deserve their own recognition; nor those being painted now in other countries, especially the USA, Canada and Australia.

Today's miniature paintings, of any subject, are being painted in different media on a variety of different surfaces, as will be seen from the illustrations in the book and explained by each of the thirty-two miniaturists.

Miniature paintings are not simply 'small pictures'. A helpful guide as to *what* they are, is that each representation, except for small creatures like bees or botanical paintings of flowers or toadstools, for example, should be not more than one-sixth of the size of the original subject. A person's head in a portrait must not exceed two inches in height. Also the size of the painting and permissible mounts are defined by the various miniature painting societies. Generally this means they must be 6 ins × 4½ ins or perhaps 7 ins × 5 ins, which includes the external measurement of the frame. On the other hand, a miniature may be as small as on a ring, a pendant or brooch, though there may be difficulties in submitting these for exhibitions. Certainly convex glass or mounts, which prevent the glass being in contact with watercolour, are required. Oil paintings do not need glass, although some are covered for protection. There is much debate about what is the 'correct' technique of a miniature painting. The simple answer is to study those that are accepted in the Royal Society of Miniature Painters, Sculptors and Gravers (known for convenience as the RMS), where some of the best miniature paintings in the world are on display. Their Exhibition is held each November in The Westminster Gallery, in Westminster Central Hall, opposite the famous Abbey.

The technique of 'stippling and hatching' referred to in the text, may not be obvious except under magnification, but the skill of the artists is evident. Not every miniaturist 'stipples and hatches', but the workmanship will be faultless, sometimes defeating the spectator's belief as to what is possible. The various glazes, described lucidly by Suzanne Lucas, PRMS, are what give the luminous quality of the watercolour miniatures.

These miniatures are called 'painting in little', but the details of the grass, the petals, the fur or other subject matter, is meticulously handled. The colours and composition, the tonal values, not forgetting the emotional content of each painting, all contribute to the beauty of the whole as a work of art. The attractive quality of a miniature from a distance is as important as that of the closest inspection, even under magnification.

Most of the miniaturists during the 19th century were painting portraits on ivory. For some, the more prestigious medium of oil on canvas became more advantageous. However, the advent of photography threatened the continuation of portraiture, until hand-coloured photographs, completed by watercolourists, using the miniaturists' technique, made it possible for a miniature to be sold at about one-fifth of the cost of a miniature painting. True portraiture fell into a decline, but has revived considerably now.

Miniatures may appear to be highly priced. There is a popular misconception existing among some people that because a painting is small it should not cost as much as a large one. However, miniatures take a very long time to complete in spite of their small size. So if a prospective client wishes to commission a portrait, what would he expect to pay? Depending on the reputation of the artist and his or her achievements in exhibitions and awards won, the prices can vary from a few hundred pounds to a thousand or more. Some indication is given in the RMS Catalogue. It does indicate why each artist strives for awards and why it is necessary to list them. It is the artist's livelihood.

Those who have visited the miniature societies in America bring back accounts of the much greater freedom of access to help amongst miniaturists; and also a different type of membership from that which exists in this country. The explanation lies in the tradition and development of miniature painting in Britain. It was a 'secret art', passed only from father to son or between a close-knit group of people, as, for example, when Isaac Oliver was apprenticed to Nicholas Hilliard.

Many well-known Art schools do not encourage miniature painting. It is not taught in this country, except in some adult colleges or Art associations; or by individual artists such as Florence Young who teaches for occasional days or weekends at Fittleworth in Sussex. Among other tutors, all featured in the text, are: Pauline Denyer, who has sessions at West Dean, or the Earnley Concourse, both near Chichester, or at Denman College. Barbara Valentine teaches at Claverham Community College in Sussex and Joan Joyce at Missenden Abbey, Great Missenden, for various sessions. Programmes are available by application to the colleges.

One point worth noting is that in miniature painting copies of old photographs or the work of other artists is permitted even in the RMS, as it has always been traditional that travellers, in particular, on long coach journeys enjoyed taking with them miniature paintings of their favourite pictures or portraits. For example, a copy of a well-known miniature, the 'Unknown Woman' by Isaac Oliver (provided acknowledgement is given), could be exhibited unless copies are specifically 'not accepted'. Many miniaturists today are not happy with submitting work that is not entirely original, and various art societies do not accept copies.

However, many beautiful miniature paintings pay tribute to the early miniaturists or Victorian ones, and do have an educative value as well. Since so many of them are in private collections or museums, they may not be so easily discovered in these days, when the cost of travel is so great. The same may be said of miniatures depicting copies from famous paintings that may be on exhibition in this country for a brief time, such as those in the Winterhalter Exhibition at the National Portrait Gallery in London two years ago. It is important, though, that the original source is acknowledged, even in the case of a magazine photograph of a well-known personality or superb photograph, such as is often portrayed on the cover of *The Lady*. Photographs taken by the artist are a considerable aid to memory, but it must be remembered that the colours and tones may be inaccurate.

The modern miniaturist should know about the techniques and surfaces on which any particular miniaturist painted, say in the 16th or 18th century, so as to give as faithful a rendering as possible. It is one of the pleasures of a miniaturist to be able to reproduce for himself an 'antique' miniature painting, when the original may have been auctioned and realised £20,000 to £30,000 or more. Studying the early masters then becomes very worthwhile and teaches so much too.

Many books are also available. Daphne Foskett's 'Miniatures Dictionary and Guide' is excellent source material. She is universally acknowledged as an expert on miniatures and 'has for years advised museums, collectors and auction houses', about them. Her book, which one hopes every library will keep, provides excellent information for those wishing to study the subject, as well as some fine colour reproductions.

The collection of portrait miniatures in the Fitzwilliam Museum, in Cambridge, is one of the finest in the country. No other public collection except that in the Victoria and Albert Museum in London, can equal its representation of the British School. The collection starts with art in this country (c.1525) and continues through the next four centuries. All the greatest British miniaturists are represented, as well as a number of leading continental artists.

Frequently in looking at miniatures, past or present, it is of enormous interest to know who the sitter is. The 'subject', be it he or she, may be famous in history or in the theatrical world. The miniature painting of Dame Peggy Ashcroft on the cover here, is recording the prominence of one of the greatest British actresses of our present era. Other miniaturists, such as W. P. Mundy, depict members of the Royal Family with his miniatures of HRH The Duke of Edinburgh and HRH Prince Charles, which is all part of 'our history'.

The identity of the sitters in the past is often not known. It might be, as one historian suggested, that Shakespeare could have been painted in miniature, but so far he has not been identified. However, we owe our knowledge of Elizabethan costumes and jewellery, hair styles and the symbolism in paintings, to the limners, as the miniaturists were called in the 16th and 17th centuries.

The illuminated manuscripts provided the name, limner; the Latin word has the same root as 'illuminating'. The modern word 'miniature' is derived from the Latin word 'minium', the red lead that provided the technical base used in manuscripts. There has been confusion sometimes with the Latin word 'minuere' (to diminish), which has no connection with the word 'miniature'. It was only in the 17th century that the small portraits were called miniatures.

It seems generally accepted that the art of miniature painting originated from the illuminated manuscripts, which were executed on parchment or vellum. The miniature paintings became an art form in their own right from their small portraits and decorations, and the artists prepared their own pigment. Phoebe Sholto Douglas tells us that by the late 16th and early 17th century, up to 35 different pigments were in use.

Miniatures can be divided, generally, into two classes: ornamental miniatures are those that are circular or oval, often encased in lockets and studded with jewels and worn as ornaments. Cabinet miniatures are oval or rectangular and are in frames to hang on walls or stand on a flat surface.

Holbein is customarily considered to be the earliest well-known painter connected with miniatures, though it is thought he learned about them from Lucas Hornebolte, who came from Ghent. Daphne Foskett in her book *Portrait Miniatures* relates an amusing story about Holbein, who was privately painting some lady's picture for King Henry VIII when a 'nobleman forced himself upon them'. Holbein threw him down the stairs before panicking and rushing to the King to beg for pardon, without saying what he had done. The King agreed to pardon him if he told the truth, but later regretted his decision somewhat.

When the nobleman arrived to complain about Holbein, the King rebuked him and reminded him that he should 'censor Holbein no further', reminding the nobleman that he, the King, could create 'many Lords out of peasants, but not one Holbein'.

A famous example of one of Holbein's miniatures is that of Anne of Cleeves, when she was being considered as a wife for Henry. It is often reproduced and is now in the Victoria and Albert Museum.

Further back in history, as a serious patron of the arts, Henry VII brought many Flemish artists to England as there was no particular tradition for small portrait paintings, as there was in Ghent. There was considerable movement across the Channel, which accounts for Nicholas Hilliard, who was born in Exeter (1547-1619) being in Germany as a boy, to avoid persecution of the Protestants when Mary Tudor came to the throne in 1553. His father, Richard Hilliard, was later a prominent goldsmith in Exeter, from whom his son Nicholas learned his skills. Nicholas, who was to become traditionally one of Britain's greatest miniature painters, was (according to Daphne Foskett) painting miniatures by the age of thirteen before serving his apprenticeship.

The early ones are in the manner of Holbein, but his style was essentially decorative. He loved painting bejewelled costumes and is said to have painted all of Queen Elizabeth's jewels. Roy Strong, in his excellent book, *The English Renaissance Miniature*, tells us that Hilliard's method for creating counterfeit stones was to mix the transparent pigments needed, using crimson lake for rubies, verdigris for emeralds and lapis lazuli for sapphires with a small amount of turpentine resin. This was taken up with a heated point and laid over the burnished silver ground. So realistic were they that they could be mistaken for the real jewels.

In painting the costumes, he emphasized the standard crispness of lace ruffs by drawing their complicated tracery with a very full brush of white lead, 'dribbling' the paint onto the surface. When magnified 'it looks like icing sugar piped by a confectioner'.

During the 16th century the emphasis was on body-colour (or pigment colour), while late in the 17th century gouache replaced body-colour. Then later in the century the tendency was for white to be added to the transparent modelling colours of the features and opaque gouache was used to heighten even the half tones of the flesh.

Towards the end of the 16th century, Hilliard invented a background which imitated folded crimson satin. The folds were shown by dragging a dry brush producing the highlights. The wet in wet technique was used. The contour of the figure would be outlined using a fine brush and a watery mixture of blue, before using the same colour with a larger brush to wash over the background. While it was still wet, another brush, with a thicker mixture of colour, would be applied, to 'lye smoth as glass'.

The flesh colour 'carnation', as it was called (which was the initial wash painted on the face of the portrait, preceding the stippling and glazing to follow), used by Hilliard and Oliver, was much paler than that of preceding miniaturists. They kept a number of vellum-covered cards prepared with various carnation hues so that they would only need to choose the one that approximated to the colouring of the sitter.

The laying of the carnation, composed of white paint with traces of other colours and diluted with water, was important for the success of the portrait. The carnation covered an area larger than that needed, and matched the smoothness and colour as nearly as possible. Sadly the features of Hilliard's portraits have faded because of the fugitive quality of the red lakes like Alizarin crimson.

He always used his disciplined hatching for modelling features. Hilliard, with his goldsmith's background, used gold to encircle the metallic lines round his work; he did the inscriptions with thick gold powder mixed with gum, and then polished them with the teeth of small animals. Burnished silver was also used in the highlights of pearls; the main body of the pearl was raised with a thick blob of white. Often Hilliard's miniatures have been marred by the deterioration of the silver.

The tentative beginnings of this new approach to the portrait miniature can be seen in the works of Peter Oliver and John Hoskins, but further innovations were made by Samuel Cooper between 1640 and 1670.

These are but a few facts about the development of the early miniaturists, to whom the modern miniaturist looks for knowledge about their techniques. The wide range of subjects now being painted by the modern miniature painters only came about relatively recently. The portrait miniature virtually disappeared with the advent of photography. But over the last decade interest in the miniature has had a most welcome revival, both from the point of view of the artist, whose unique skills are being appreciated, and for the collectors, who are appreciating them as heirlooms of the future. It is a sample of these artists to whom the author pays tribute.

THE SUBJECTS of the ARTISTS

(Artists listed alphabetically in the book)

LANDSCAPES	Oil on copper	W. Burdett-Somers ARMS MAA HS
	Watercolour	Loveda Cox HS
	Oil on board	Robert Hughes RMS HS
	Watercolour	Meg Kingston HS
	Watercolour	Eric Morton ARMS HS
	Watercolour	Rosalind Pierson RMS HS
	Watercolour	Sheila Sanford RI RMS
	Watercolour	Florence Young RMS SWA
PORTRAITS	Watercolour	Margaret Adams ARMS HS
	Watercolour	Phyllis Arnold RMS PUSM PUSWA SM HS FIBA
	Pencil on Paper	Jenny Brooks HS
	Watercolour	Jennifer Buxton RMS HS
	Watercolour	Pauline Denyer SLm Des.RCA HS
	Watercolour	Elaine H. Fellows ARMS SWA HS USM
	Watercolour	W. P. Mundy RMS FSCD HS
	Watercolour	Margaret Ryder VPRMS SWA FSBA HS SM
	Watercolour	Phoebe Sholto Douglas RMS HS
	Watercolour	Sydney Shorthouse RMS HS
ACTORS	Watercolour	Barbara Valentine NDD ARMS SLm
FLOWERS	Acrylic	Pamela Davis VPRMS FSBA SWA HS
	Oil	Sheila Fairman RMS FSBA SWA HS
	Watercolour	Suzanne Lucas FLS PRMS FSBA SWA Hon.HS
	Watercolour	Margaret Ryder VPRMS SWA FSBA HS SM
DUTCH FLOWERS	Watercolour	Barbara Valentine NDD ARMS SLm
SEASCAPES	Watercolour	Cdr. G. W. G. Hunt RN ARMS HS
ANIMALS	Watercolour	Heather O. Catchpole RMS HS
	Oil on Ivorine	Sheila Fairman RMS FSBA SWA
	Watercolour	Daphne Lee RMS HS
BIRDS	Watercolour	Joyce Rogerson RMS SWA HS MASF USM
	Watercolour	Eric Morton ARMS HS
BUILDINGS	Watercolour	Maureen Pearson HS
INTERIORS	Watercolour	C. Elisabeth M. Lake RMS HS
STILL LIFE	Oil on ivorine	Sheila Fairman RMS FSBA SWA HS
ILLUMIN-ATIONS	Watercolour	Henry Saxon RMS HS

AWARDS

(The winners of these awards, when relevant, are given in the text)

When possible, awards won in Ulster or abroad are mentioned, but this is mainly a book to enjoy, not a comprehensive text book.

THE MAIN AWARDS OF THE ROYAL SOCIETY OF MINIATURE PAINTERS SCULPTORS AND GRAVERS are:

THE ROYAL SOCIETY OF MINIATURE PAINTERS SCULPTORS AND GRAVERS GOLD MEMORIAL BOWL. (First awarded in 1985)

The Judging Committee for the above award varies each year. It may be The President, with two experts on miniatures invited from Christie's and Sotheby's, as in 1987, or from the Victoria and Albert Museum or other expert advisers.

THE MUNDY SOVEREIGN PORTRAIT AWARD (First given in 1983)

THE MARGARET RYDER NON-MEMBER'S AWARD (First given in 1984)

THE GORDON DRUMMOND AWARD FOR MINIATURES OTHER THAN PORTRAITS (First given in 1983)

FAIRMAN MEMBER'S SUBJECT MINIATURE AWARD (First given in 1990)

THE HILLIARD SOCIETY AWARDS are:

SUZANNE LUCAS AWARD - BEST IN EXHIBITION (Abbreviated to 'Best in Exhibition' in the text. First presented by Suzanne Lucas in 1984)

SUZANNE LUCAS AWARD - BEST NOVICE AWARD (Abbreviated to 'Best Novice Award' in the text. First presented by Suzanne Lucas 1984)

THE BELL AWARD First presented in 1987 and specifically provided to encourage the art of Portrait Painting in Miniature

Please see end of book for information about some Miniature Painting Societies and 'Suppliers of Materials for Miniature Painting'.

MARGARET ADAMS

Margaret Adams lives and paints her watercolour miniatures in Dorset. At an age when most people have been retired for some time, she has achieved astonishing success in just two years. Three months after joining a newly-established class, under the auspices of the Sherborne Arts Centre Association, where she discovered her gift for miniature painting, she worked on her own before winning the Best Novice Award (shared) in 1989. Within two years of successfully submitting to the RMS, she became an associate member (ARMS). She was an inspiration to the class and her achievement has helped the class to evolve into 'The Sherborne Miniature Painting Society'. She is the first Honorary Member.

Margaret's subjects, painted in watercolour on ivorine or ivory, are based on old family photographs, before they fade. The miniature of 'Malayan Court Dancers' was in both the 1990 HS and RMS Exhibitions. In it, the delicate colours and fine stippling are in a circular painting of five inches in diameter and needed around one hundred hours of work. It was most attractive and brilliantly executed.

Until the age of eighteen she used all her spare hours experimenting with the photographic materials and techniques of that time. It is not by chance that her work is so meticulous. After a brief spell at the Farnham Art School, she went to the Bloomsbury Trade School in Queen's Square, London. There she spent one year 'spotting', retouching and finishing photographs. She did tinting and made photographic bases for miniatures. This training enabled her to take a job at Shaw Wildman's Studio. He was then the foremost photographer. They did all Kodak's advertisements for hoardings and the photography for Harrods, Vogue, Moss Bros and many others. Her task was to 'slim down', and take out blemishes on the models on 10 × 8 inch glossy prints, with a knife and watercolour. She and her colleagues were like apprentices for three years, for one pound a week. But she learned to stipple!

With the outbreak of war, that type of photography ceased; then she was 'on the land' for the duration of the War. During this time she worked for the Chief Inspector of Mechanisation, which involved photographing tanks and weapons and 'blocking out'; that meant removing factories from the photographic backgrounds of tanks.

Something that contributes to the consistency of her results is that while she is painting she makes detailed notes about her colour combinations. Like many others, she finds that in miniature painting, she experiences a stillness and meditative quality existing in few activities today.

PHYLLIS ARNOLD

Phyllis Arnold's works are in the collection of Her Majesty Queen Elizabeth II and many other eminent people. Her paintings are included in the collections of the Ulster Museum and The National Trust and similar such august commissioning bodies in Britain and Northern Ireland. She lectures on Miniatures and Silhouettes and has contributed to regional programmes for television and radio. In 1977 she was commissioned by Coalport Porcelain to paint a portrait in profile of Her Majesty the Queen, which was used on thirteen items of porcelain, mostly limited editions, to celebrate the Silver Jubilee.

She trained in Commercial Art in Belfast and is a professional artist who has been self-employed since the late Sixties. She owns and manages her Art Studio and Antiques Gallery in Bangor, Northern Ireland, where she also restores and cleans antique watercolours and miniatures. She is married with two sons.

Phyllis has exhibited at the Royal Academy Summer Exhibition, The Royal Ulster Academy, The Federation of British Artists' Permanent Exhibition 1983-84, and The British Artists' Invitation Watercolour Exhibition in 1983. In 1980, '81 and '83 she was a finalist for the Hunting Group Art Awards and Highly Commended for the RMS Gold Memorial Bowl in 1986 and winner of the Gold Memorial Bowl in 1988. She is listed in the 'Who's Who in Art' 21st Edition, 'The World's Who's Who of Women Artists' and in Peggy Hickman's 'Silhouettes, A Living Art'. Her biography will be included in the new edition of 'The Kunstler Lexikon' (known as Theme Becker) – the German published International Dictionary of Artists. Her paintings and prints of her work have been sold throughout Europe, America, Canada and the Far East.

She is interested in various styles of the earlier miniaturists and does not aim to paint a very modern image, but likes to think of her work being in the tradition of the 18th or 19th century artists. Her method is to stipple and dot to give a sense of time and atmosphere to the sitter, as well as to achieve the likeness.

Her work is divided between her painting and selling antique silhouettes and miniatures. Phyllis also has a personal collection of various artists' work, like Mrs Beetham and Eduoart, Frith and all the well-known antique silhouettists.

As there was nobody else, to her knowledge, in the Province of Ulster who was painting portrait miniatures, she now gives lessons in the art. Phyllis believes she was the first Irish artist to be a full member of the RMS.

Phyllis paints large watercolours, but her miniatures are mainly topographical buildings, houses, figurative, poultry and other farm animals and, of course, portraits. She paints on vellum, sometimes ivory, paper or a plaster surface for silhouettes in gouache paint, and works on a tilted surface.

She has a paintbox of forty-eight colours, but usually for portraits uses only about five or six, which are: Yellow Ochre, Vermillion, Light Red, Cobalt, Vandyke Brown and Raw Umber; and does not use Oxgall. Black is mainly for silhouettes with white, sometimes, for clothing.

She takes about twelve photographs of the sitter and makes colour notes and comments about the personality, clothes and so on. Then she measures up methodically from a photograph for the width between the eyes, the length and width of face, and starts to draw a likeness, taken from about three or four photographs, on to tracing paper. When she is satisfied with the sketch, she transfers it to vellum or ivory by rubbing the back faintly with a soft pencil and presses the image through. Next, she paints the outline in pale flesh colour and uses an eraser when it is dry, to remove any graphite remaining. One or two more sittings may be needed to complete the portrait.

The silhouettes are drawn from life in pencil within about ten minutes in all. When the sitter has left, she paints round the pencil outline and fills it in, adding overpainting perhaps. If it is to be on plaster, the tracing is transferred to the surface. Her silhouettes are also on pendant jewellery with gold overpainting to pick up the gold antique settings.

In 1986, Phyllis Arnold founded The Ulster Society of Miniaturists of whom there are about thirty-four members, and she is the current President, in addition to her other official roles.

JENNY BROOKS

It is surprising how frequently someone's art is just as much indication of character as is handwriting. The author imagines that this is clearly so for Jenny Brooks, whose particular medium is pencil portraits on paper. Her immaculate drawings require many hours of painstaking perseverence with a very hard pencil. They tell little of her personality, other than that she must be a most patient person and is capable of extreme concentration.

Using a light box, she traces off the main shapes from the photograph of her subject on to the paper with a 6H pencil before rubbing most of the lines away with a soft putty rubber, leaving very faint marks. Then she gradually builds up layers of shapes of different tones starting with the 9H pencil, so that the tonal structure of the drawing is built into a finished work with every area 'resolved'.

Jenny works on one area at a time, gradually moving across the picture so that the whole drawing is 'worked up' to the same set of tonal values. That process is repeated several times using softer pencils to produce the darker tones eventually.

The actual marks she makes are short diagonal hatching strokes from right to left, which can be clearly seen under a magnifying glass. She can take up to forty hours before she is satisfied that the drawing is completed.

She describes herself as a purist and perfectionist ('needing a quiet and creative atmosphere'), and this is evident in her drawings. She is very organised in setting out equipment and materials, including the best hand-made smooth HP paper and watercolour paints, before beginning her work.

Her first introduction to painting and drawing in miniature was in 1987 at an Adult Education class, but she has been painting and drawing since childhood. She had an academic training in Fine Art in the sixties at the Bath Academy of Art, at Corsham in Wiltshire. Then she continued her academic studies at Goldsmiths' College in London where she obtained a postgraduate Art Teacher's Certificate.

From 1968 to 1978 she taught Art and became Head of the Art Department at Blackheath Bluecoat Church of England mixed comprehensive school in London. In 1990 she became a part-time Lecturer in Fine Art at Brunel College in Bristol, and in Fine Art, Miniature Painting and Botanical Painting; and Drawing in Adult Education.

She exhibited her work locally in Bristol, near where she lives, and at the RMS in 1989 and 1990. She won the 'Best Novice Award' at the

Hilliard Society in 1990 for her portrait of her step-son Quinton. There is every indication that she will continue to win awards.

She took two years to develop her Fine Art Portraiture and Design business successfully. She specializes in landscape, architectural, animal and botanical subjects to commission, besides portraits. She is now well-known for her careful execution and quality of detail.

Her portraits began when a colleague at Riddlesworth Hall School in Norfolk asked her for an exhibition for parents' day and this led to commissions from all the children in the class on behalf of the parents. She spent eight years there running the Art and Craft department, before moving to the West Country.

In 1987 she was self-employed as a free-lance artist, and from 1988-89 she combined free-lance work with teaching Painting and Drawing at Backwell Comprehensive School. She was married at the Quaker Meeting House in Diss in Norfolk and her husband is in management.

It is evident she has worked hard at her teaching, which she says she enjoys enormously, and her own skills, for which she is deservedly winning recognition.

WILHELMINA BURDETT-SOMERS

Wilhelmina was born in The Hague and received her first formal Art training at the Netherlands Royal Academy. She married and came to live in Louth, Lincolnshire in 1964, where she has continued with her painting.

She began miniature oil painting on copper in 1966. 1978 was the first year in which her miniatures were accepted at the RMS and also her first venture to the USA, when four miniatures were shown at El Centro, California, and were awarded a first and a second place.

In 1980 she had her first contact with the Florida Miniature Art Society, followed by a developing connection with other American Art Societies in New Jersey and Washington. She became a member of all of them and has exhibited annually with them.

She held her own private exhibition of sixty landscape miniatures in Queen's Gate Place in London in 1981, and in the Academy Summer Exhibition in 1984 her miniature of Worcester Cathedral was accepted and sold. That year she was awarded their 'Award of Highest Merit' in Florida and two awards in Washington, DC. That was all the more interesting because of a visit arranged to The White House, to inspect the collection of miniatures held permanently there.

In 1986 a miniature of Truro Cathedral gained the Grumbacher Gold Medal Award in the sixteenth International Art Exhibition in New Jersey.

Wilhelmina has exhibited and sold her miniatures at the RMS since 1978 and was awarded ARMS in 1983. She has also exhibited annually at the Hilliard Society since 1982. Now she has been invited to join the prestigious Miniature Artists of America Society, which only accept award winners in the American Societies, and she is now entitled to be a Signature Member: MAA.

Wilhelmina's paintings are full of colour, which can be accounted for by her love of the changing colours of the skies and her great admiration for Turner. Her 'Cathedral' paintings are very memorable and have proved artistically successful, and also record many of our beautiful buildings. Her painting of Lincoln Cathedral, reproduced later, gives an excellent idea of her work.

PORTRAITS ANIMALS WATERCOLOUR ON IVORY OTHER MEDIA ON OTHER SURFACES

JENNIFER BUXTON

Jennifer always wanted to draw people. Her sister and their dog were the most frequent models. Then she learned the techniques of watercolour and oil painting and pastel from Marguerite Frobisher in a weekly lesson from the age of eleven.

She won a scholarship to the Byam Shaw School of Art at sixteen, but found the school, for her, discouraged individuality and insisted that students should 'paint big'! Jennifer says that her small watercolour sketches of fellow students were her best work at that time.

After art school and marriage to Vic she began doing pastel pictures of dogs and cats, and occasionally people. When her son was small someone suggested she should try miniature painting in the evening from photographs, as her husband was away at sea. It was immediately apparent that painting in detail on ivory was fascinating and exciting and she worked hard to improve her technique. She discovered that she was using the paint too dry and too strong in colour at first. Then Boyd Waters, a miniature painter who was blind and dying, gave her some help. After his death his widow, Mildred, gave her his beautiful Parisian miniature easel box, which provided the inspiration and opportunity to study his work. She imagined he was helping her to paint. The top of the box opens to form a slope and the ivory rests securely on the soft material inset into the slope. She copied the portrait of a little French girl, which helped her improve her own work.

Jennifer preferred to paint from life, but as it was not always possible she developed her own way of working from a pastel sketch done from life and using black and white photographs, which she developed and printed herself. She used a one hundred millimetre lens to avoid distortion. She arranged the photographs and pastels around her and then painted freely with a light mixture of cobalt and light red onto the ivory. Placing the head in the oval, she roughly sketched in the hair and clothes first using No. 1 and No. 2 Diana Kilinsky sable brushes, gradually changing to smaller ones. Next, she washed in a flesh tint of yellow and rose madder across the face, making it warmer near the cheeks, nose and chin. Then came a wash of colour across the background, the clothes and the hair, probably dropping some stronger colour into the hair while the highlight colour was still wet. She would try to place the iris of the eyes and start the shadows on the face with a mix of the flesh tone and a little cobalt blue and, sometimes, cerulean blue with some burnt sienna around the mouth.

A gradual increase of colour and tone everywhere, done with fine strokes or dots of quite liquid paint, would strengthen the painting, keeping it all going as a whole. Paint once down is left to dry; if it needs altering it can be lifted off with a brush and clean water. She would give the eyes the most attention; a person looks out of his eyes and if they are not right the likeness will not come. She believes the eyes should be the most detailed part of the portrait as they draw the attention of the viewer.

Usually, she only uses water with the paint, but if the surface does not seem receptive she sometimes uses an egg emulsion. She takes the yolk of an egg and lets it drop into a clean jar leaving the skin in the palm of her hand to be discarded. She mixes some water with the yolk, shakes it well and takes a small amount to give the paint more substance and bite. Halfway through the painting the surface is inclined to look dirty and it is easy to think all is not well. However, perseverance and steady work create a transformation; gradually the skin starts to glow and a most wonderful feeling comes, 'as if she is removing veils of mist to reveal the sitter', or 'as if she were a medium through whom the personality of the sitter could manifest himself upon the ivory'.

Sometimes she paints on Kelmscott vellum, which is a lovely surface, but she found that she needed to stroke it with the froth of a well beaten egg white to give it a good surface on which to work. Colours stay strong and pure, but the flesh does not have the same translucence as it would if painted on ivory.

After twenty-five years of lovingly painting miniature portraits, her eyesight deteriorated slightly and she needed spectacles and a magnifying glass. She no longer felt the same joy in it and painting became a struggle. She believes people should only paint 'small', if that is what they sincerely believe is the right size for the work; so when this was no longer true for her she stopped painting portraits in miniature, except occasionally.

Although it is a great honour to win awards it does not bestow an easy life or a sense of pride. An artist, especially a portrait painter, is only as good as the painting he or she is doing at the time. Each new portrait presents the same and different problems. The same or different mistakes can be made; each painting requires full commitment, concentration, endeavour and hard work, with a willingness to let the painting develop into an interpretation of the living spirit of the sitter.

This wonderful advice is given by Jennifer who, in 1985 at the Inaugural Presentation at the RMS, and who was Honorary Secretary at the time, was awarded the Gold Memorial Bowl for her portrait of Winifred Beeby RMS (the maiden name of Suzanne Lucas' mother, Lydia Craven).

HEATHER O. CATCHPOLE

by Jo Clay and Heather O. Catchpole

Heather Catchpole works at her home in the Somerset village of Fitzhead, where she and her husband live with their two cocker spaniels. Originally from Vancouver Island, part of British Columbia in Canada, she trained in Graphic Arts in Durban, South Africa, and worked in Johannesburg in the 1960s before coming to England.

Already enjoying a successful career in pastel portraiture, she began painting miniatures after her first visit to the RMS Exhibition in 1979. Heather gladly acknowledges, too, that she owes a great debt of thanks to Jennifer Buxton, for advice and every encouragement in those early days of 'a door being opened on a new and wonderful world'. As a fine portraitist Heather has made many friends all over the world through this very personal form of art. Because of her natural love for animals she thoroughly enjoys dog portraiture and has the ability to capture their individual personalities. This is much appreciated by the owners of these 'sitters' who are often quite emotional about the portraits of their pets.

As a conservationist she will not countenance the use of ivory so Heather's miniatures are always painted on ivorine. Her watercolour palette consists of around twelve colours with, sometimes, a little gouache. Work begins with a collection of detailed drawings, colour notes and her own photographs, all having been taken while enabling the sitter to relax; and observing her while making thumbnail sketches on layout paper. All are of the same size as the finished portrait, from which the final one is chosen and then completed in fine detail. A firm dark outline ensures the drawing can be seen when the ivorine is placed over it; a light-box is invaluable for this. With a finely pointed brush the drawing is traced on to the ivorine in a watercolour line of a light warm grey or similar. No pencil-work is done directly on to the ivorine. Painting with a brush that has enough body to hold a fair amount of paint, as well as having a good point, she begins with an initial light tonal wash of the basic colours, which is allowed to dry completely. The painting is built up with stippling or hatching, depending on the desired finished effect. Finally, having put the work away for a few days, she views her work with a fresh eye and adds any necessary finishing touches.

Every portrait has information inside the frame recording the sitter's name, place and date of birth (often confidential), name of artist and so forth; also stating any exhibitions in which the portrait has been shown.

It is an interesting exercise on how colours react to light, when a sheet of ivorine marked with all her colours is exposed to light on her studio windowsill for any length of time. This results, sometimes, in banishing some favourites. Other tips include: waterjars with lids to keep dust out, a kitchen-roll, which does not leave 'flecks' like other types of tissue, and for erasing, a minute piece of putty-rubber held in tweezers is invaluable.

Heather's interest in miniatures includes the history of English Portrait Miniatures on which she gives talks. Silhouettes and their history is another of her themes. She travels extensively and her work is now in many countries in the world.

SYLVIA CAVE

Sylvia attended the Byam Shaw School of Art in London and obtained an Honours degree in Archaeology and Fine Art at Edinburgh University. She then spent ten years in art publishing in New York City.

Since 1977 she has made a living in Britain as a freelance painter and teacher. A particular fascination with the jewel-like qualities of wild flowers, lichens, insects and reptiles led her naturally to miniature painting. She is a particularly enthusiastic champion of reptiles, creatures of great charm and beauty, frequently given an undeservedly bad reputation.

Sylvia paints miniatures on vellum because of the special glow it gives to colours and the fine detail that can be achieved. The variations of texture and tone on the surface of the vellum can also give interesting backgrounds. Watercolours, both transparent and opaque, are used. Another more unorthodox technique involves picking out only part of the design in colour; for instance, it may be the animal depicted, whilst leaving the rest as a fine pencil drawing.

It is invaluable to spend time on working sketches out-of-doors and doing more detailed studies in the studio. This also builds a useful collection of reference material, which can be used for a finished painting when a particular plant is out of season or an animal not available. She draws the design for a miniature very loosely at first on tracing paper with the detail gradually worked up. The finished drawing is transferred to the vellum as a very faint outline, which gives plenty of scope for fresh ideas in the painting. The design is then picked out in a delicate flat or tonal under-painting. Colour, tone, texture and detail are carefully built up with ultra-fine line or stipple. It is essential to keep the paint clean and bright at all stages.

Sylvia acknowledges the invaluable help and support Heather Catchpole has given her in the study of miniature painting, and is fortunate enough to live in Williton, near Taunton, not far from Heather. Sylvia is a most charming person and as a teacher must be very popular.

LANDSCAPES ANIMALS BIRDS LIFE DRAWINGS VARIOUS MEDIA

LOVEDA COX

For several years Loveda had been painting small watercolours, then a course at the Berkshire College of Art gave her the stimulus she needed, while her daughters were growing up. Then in 1985 she became particularly interested in painting miniatures.

The surface she prefers to paint on is watercolour paper hot pressed, board or ivorine, and she enjoys experimenting with egg tempera and acrylics. She tackles most subjects including some portraits and flowers, and has a particular eye for imaginative activities such as a cat prowling purposefully as it stalks a quarry; or a cow contemplating nature, with a bird perched on its back.

Over the years she has achieved considerable success. As a result of her miniature paintings on sale in various Oxford galleries or others nearby, she was invited to join the SWA, and regularly exhibits in the delightful small gallery in Tetsworth in Oxfordshire. She also has local exhibitions in Wallingford, where she lives. In 1989 she had three paintings accepted at the RMS and also exhibited with the Hilliard Society. In 1990 she had a miniature accepted by the Oxford Art Society, overcoming their reluctance, it seems, to accept miniatures. Until recently, this attitude was commonplace for many galleries or exhibitions, but now the barriers are coming down: the pattern is changing.

It is a credit to the quality of Loveda's work that she is constantly 'stretching' herself, never being satisfied to rest on past achievements.

She finds she is learning all the time and studies as widely as possible the different techniques and historical details of the early miniatures; and she particularly enjoys the illuminated manuscripts. She finds an obsession for perfection, combined with frustration and delight in her efforts, drives her continuously to aim for perfection.

Now that her daughters are more independent, she paints for about four hours a day. She also loves walking and gardening, both of which act as an inspiration for her paintings.

She uses Winsor and Newton's Artist Quality Watercolours some of the time, and 'le franc and bourgeois', so as to have different colours to use. Both models and photographs are source-material for her work. Often a complete painting comes to mind and seems to grow from 'thin air'. Hopefully it will do so for a long time.

PAMELA DAVIS

Three years of formal Art school training together with experience in a commercial studio, followed by many years of free-lance work, gave Pamela Davis the excellent foundation she needed for the Art world. Her painting is now entirely given to subjects of her own choice. As a miniaturist, she is self-taught.

She experimented with several media and surfaces, but now paints mainly with acrylics on ivorine and board. A constant search for new subjects has enlarged her range of work, and her extensive experience has gained her a variety of awards. These include being a finalist in the prestigious Hunting Group Art Prizes each year from 1982-84, and in 1987 she was awarded 'Best in Exhibition' at the Hilliard Society. For six consecutive years, 1985 to 1990, she achieved the distinction of an Honourable Mention in the 'Gold Memorial Bowl Award' at the RMS Exhibition.

Pamela Davis is one of the three Vice-Presidents of the RMS, where she exhibits in their annual November Exhibition and various galleries both in this country and abroad. The author has admired her work in the Medici Galleries and in the Llewellyn Alexander (Fine Arts) Gallery. Painting miniatures is, for Pamela, not only sheer delight but an all-absorbing obsession.

Her choice of acrylic paints reflects her need to represent the brilliance of the colours in the flowers portrayed; the yellow in primroses or pinks and reds in strawberries are so realistic. The acrylics provide all the tints and hues needed.

Some people find difficulty working in the medium because of the fast-drying quality of the paint on the palette. The method used to overcome this problem is quite simply solved by using a shallow container, which will hold a small amount of water, in conjunction with a stay-wet palette refill made by Rowneys. A sheet of this can be cut to size, placed in the base of the tray and kept damp while in use. Paint retained on this surface will remain workable for several hours.

Any of the normal surfaces used for miniature paintings can be used, but Pamela recommends experimenting with others. The advantage of discovering a ground that is particularly suited to the individual is an unexpected bonus. Ivorine gives a translucent appearance which is most attractive and it accepts the paint well. Paper is equally adaptable, but some types of paper are more suitable for the artist's requriements. Bristol Board offers a firm ground and good surface without being too thick or heavy.

Having experimented with various makes and sizes of brushes, she finds a No. 4 sable holds sufficient paint to cover all types of painting from board backgrounds to the smallest detail. She does not favour the 0 range of brushes usually used by miniaturists. After use the brush must be washed well and the point carefully re-set to be used again.

She paints directly on to the surface and says if a pencil must be used for the design, a fairly hard H one diminishes the amount of graphite, which may otherwise penetrate the paint and reduce the brilliance of the artist's work, which is of primary importance to Pamela.

In painting miniatures, the first stage is the layout and blocking in of the subject, executed with the thinnest dilution of burnt umber and a little Rowney's Cryla Medium No. 2. The thin paint allows for any alterations necessary. An indication of where the subject is placed should now be apparent. Next, the very dark areas are established and the dark and light tones are gradually added.

The background, if there is one, is painted at this point; next, the colours are overpainted as necessary, with the minimum of mixing; the colours are then strengthened until the final details and highlights complete the painting.

Another advantage of acrylics is that they do not require a glass cover. An unglazed painting can be varnished. The framing, she says, can give an individual stamp to an artist's work. As an expert in the medium, who could give better advice? She is also a fine artist and knows how to impart the knowledge to others.

PAULINE DENYER

It is no surprise that Pauline Denyer received an RMS Memorial Gold Bowl Honourable Mention at the RMS Exhibition in 1990. She served a valuable apprenticeship for her chosen field of Miniature Painting, which is portraiture. Her portrait of 'Mother Theresa' and 'Portrait of Shelley', in the 1990 Hilliard Society Exhibition in May at Wells, drew special attention; while those of 'Sir John Gielgud' and 'Dame Peggy Ashcroft', were much admired in November at the RMS Exhibition at the Westminster Gallery in the Westminster Central Hall, that year.

She is versatile enough to enjoy painting animals, which she does equally well, but wants to avoid being categorized as an animal painter. Her work is most sensitive, yet has an attractive strength and individuality gained from her training in Fine Art, for two years, at the Brighton College of Art. She studied portraiture and costume with the late Charles Knight, whom she credits with much she learned. She then took the National Diploma in Design for a further two years, specialising in Fashion, and visited Paris regularly to see the Collections.

In 1961, she gained a place in the Fashion School at the Royal College of Art. During her time there, she learned how to represent textures, cloth, fur and jewellery in her designs.

It was the best time to be at the RCA. Ozzie Clarke was in her year and Zandra Rhodes in the Textile School. Janey Ironside was Professor of Fashion Design.

Pauline married in 1964, graduated from the RCA in 1965 and worked in the 'rag trade' to complete her training. She did not enjoy the commercial angle of that business as there was so little time for artistic designing. With the arrival of her first child, she was glad to leave that work behind, but was asked to teach aspects of Fashion Design at Brighton and also at Worthing, which she continued to do until the early Seventies. Pauline relished those years, as she was again working in an atmosphere of Art and Design.

She continued to teach in Adult Education during the Seventies and in 1980 decided to return to Fine Art. For this, she took some courses in Miniature Painting with Elizabeth Davys Wood and Pauline naturally found her previous experience invaluable; as has the study of the old miniatures in the Victoria and Albert Museum in London. She studied Vermeer's paintings especially and likes to combine the tight style of John Smart with the looseness of Vermeer or Frans Hals, so as to cultivate her own style. She is also influenced by Charles Rennie Mackintosh's watercolour technique, and would like to develop her own ideas with his influence.

PORTRAITS (WATERCOLOUR OR OILS)
ENAMEL ON COPPER WATERCOLOUR ON VELLUM

PHOEBE SHOLTO DOUGLAS

Mrs Phoebe Sholto Douglas is featured in Daphne Foskett's 'Miniatures Dictionary and Guide', in which her delightful 4½ inch high oval portrait on ivory of Clare Whitaker is reproduced in black and white. To achieve such recognition is notable, as she had little formal education in Art. She spent one year at the old Eastbourne College of Art from 1923/24, but was never taught how to paint miniatures. She 'just started' and read all she could about them.

Her first miniature in 1940 was of her husband's grandfather from an old photograph, and for two or three years she painted for pleasure before she began exhibiting her paintings. As a member of the RMS, she exhibited with them for about ten years, before being awarded an associate membership (ARMS) in 1970, and becoming a full member (RMS) two years later.

As the daughter of an artist (and since there were four generations of artists in the family), she decided to become an artist early in life and used to hang her work on furniture and charge adults to 'view' them! Her father, Lawson Wood, was a well-known artist in his time and his work has now become fashionable again, she says. As a boy, Sydney Shorthouse, RMS, remembers him vividly, and credits Phoebe's father with having influenced him more than any other artist. Her painting of her father at work is reproduced here, with that of her mother. Rather charmingly, she regards the production of the book and the inclusion of the portraits of her parents as a permanent tribute to them.

She never copies from other miniatures, but enjoys adapting old photographs to miniature paintings, no doubt as a result of working for four years with the photographer Gilbert Adams after spending nine years in commercial art and advertising. She painted miniatures on a photographic base for him and felt that those people from past generations 'came alive' for her. She is always adapting new ideas and exploring different territory in her painting.

Phoebe has used oil paints on ivory or ivorine, but prefers watercolour on ivory, ivorine or vellum. Apart from portraits, she paints birds, animals, still-life and imaginative subjects as well as enamelling on copper.

A few years ago she had an interesting commission, to produce twenty-five bird pictures in enamel ovals of 1″ × 1½″, to be incorporated in the binding of a book of poetry and prose for the Nottingham Court Press.

Phoebe was educated privately and later married Keith Sholto Douglas, now deceased. She became Head of the Art Department of Bethany School in Goudhurst in Kent, where she still lives. She exhibits with the RMS, RI, RA and SWA and on several occasions at the Royal Academy Summer Exhibitions, also at the Christchurch Centenary Exhibition in New Zealand, as well as having her own exhibitions in local galleries as a Portrait Miniature Painter.

Besides her painting, Phoebe has written a six-part series covering the History of Miniature Painting in the *Artist* magazine some years ago. She describes lucidly the origin of the art and follows it through from the Early Masters to the present day. She explains that Dudley Heath in his book 'Miniatures', published in 1905, divides the art of miniature painting into four distinct schools, the first of which flourished under the Tudor dynasty of the 15th and 16th centuries. Then came the Stuarts of the 17th century, the Georgians of the 18th century and that of the 'present day', which for him was the Victorian era. We can add the 20th century to his list. It is a very helpful treatise for anyone wishing to place miniature painting in its historical context and for a basis on which to build for the miniature painters practising today. The author found the features most interesting. Mrs Sholto Douglas explained the background history clearly and succinctly.

To quote a fellow artist, Sydney Shorthouse, 'She is the most delightful of gentle ladies', as well as being so gifted.

SHEILA FAIRMAN

Sheila Fairman studied at the Southend-on-Sea Art College. She started painting miniatures in 1977 after visiting the RMS the previous year, where she was extremely impressed by the range and quality of work. With her love of painting fine details it seemed to be the perfect challenge, and she began experimenting in oil (her usual medium) on fine canvas. Later she was given some ivorine and discovered oil works well on this surface. Even better, it has a special quality that gives a luminosity similar to that of ivory.

Between 1973 and 1976, she concentrated on painting shells and feathers, and exhibited work at the Royal Society of Marine Artists and for three years at the Royal Academy. She also enjoys painting larger pictures, many featuring her favourite subjects, such as the 'swirling pattern of dough in a Chelsea bun, or the texture of a custard tart with its crisp pastry. Do people really look at the everyday objects of life' she asks, 'such as the texture of the skin of clementines or the skin of mushrooms? Or is it only artists who appreciate this sort of detail?'

Her miniature paintings have won many awards. She was a prizewinner in the Hunting Group Art Prizes for British Artists in 1982, and a finalist in 1981 and 1983. In 1985, she won the HS Best in Exhibition and the Gordon Drummond Award for the 'Best Miniature Other Than Portraits', in the RMS exhibition. In the 1989 RMS exhibition, she was awarded the Gold Memorial Bowl for a painting of plums with a wonderfully realistic 'bloom' that made them seem most tempting. It is an art she has perfected.

The *Leisure Painter* has been innovative in accepting features, over the years, by eminent artists including Sheila Fairman, Margaret Ryder and W. P. Mundy (all in this book). One of the features Sheila wrote gave explicit information about how to paint on ivorine. In the illustration of her Chelsea buns, the sugar on top gleams with light and beside it a raisin has fallen away. A bite by human teeth, etching out the edges of custard tarts or buns, is so evocative as to be mouthwatering.

She explains it very simply. The top of the buns are painted with raw sienna, burnt sienna and burnt umber with a touch of alizarin, built up in thin layers of paint, which is 'glazing'. A final glazing of Indian Yellow is added. The white of the crystalline sugar is toned down with blues and greys, with only an occasional touch of pure white where a crystal catches the light.

She begins by laying down all the foundation colours, except the background which she leaves until last, in case the outer areas of the painting become smudged. The layers of this colour are built up, which gives the depth and richness of colours, especially in the darker colours. A brush with a thicker point achieves the sharper definitions in lighter areas, particularly the highlights; working on the shadows at the same time ensures the correct compatibility of tones. Sheila reminds us that the shadows reflect the colour of the subject as does the interplay of reflections between the two objects. Then the background is added on the non-absorbent surface of the ivorine. She waits a week for the paint to dry before framing the painting.

They are displayed in Robert Wood's fine gold-rimmed, velvet-backed frames (marketed as R.J.W. Products), as are many of the RMS paintings. Her brushes are sable, ranging in size from 2 to 000, the latter being used only for fine details. In designing a picture she reminds us that the spaces are as important as the subject itself and the shadows can be a vital part of the painting.

One tip she gives for painting a seascape is to apply the foundation colours with a soft rag, before superimposing the cloud formations. Tiny blobs of lighter colour create a shimmering effect on the water. The amount of sky reflected in the water is dictated by weather conditions. It is distorted by choppy or rough seas, and is almost mirrored in calm water. Sheila can teach us all about the importance of minute observation and makes us smile when she exhibits such originality as hers at the Hilliard Society and RMS.

ELAINE H. FELLOWS

In 1981 Elaine Fellows was awarded an Honours Degree in Visual Communications and then worked as a designer for a museum before becoming an illustrator for various advertising agencies. She painted mainly architectural subjects on a larger scale of about 10″ × 8″, but did not feel at ease with that size so began reducing it. She painted her first miniature in watercolour on a paper base in 1986. The same year she submitted work to the RMS for the first time and was accepted. It was there she discovered ivorine, which inevitably altered her technique.

She joined the Hilliard Society in 1986 and was accepted as a full exhibiting member in 1987. She began painting professionally in 1988, when she was invited to join the SWA and awarded Full Membership in the same year. She continued to exhibit her work with the RMS and was awarded an associate membership (ARMS) in 1989, when she was also given an Honourable Mention for the Gold Memorial Bowl Award.

She won the 'Bell Award for Portraiture' in 1990 at the Hilliard Society, for 'The Toast', a painting of a blue-costumed gentleman holding an elegant long glass of red wine. In March 1991, she was Highly Commended for the 'Ulster Savings Perpetual Trophy' for a still life subject, 'The Plough', and won the 'Madam MacCarthy Mór Memorial Award for Portraiture', in the Ulster Society of Miniaturists' Exhibition. Now she regularly exhibits work with galleries, mainly in London. The Llewellyn Alexander (Fine Paintings) Ltd. is especially proud to exhibit her work.

When working on vellum, Elaine likes to follow the methods of Nicholas Hilliard as much as possible. A study of his work introduced her to the flat blue background using the wet in wet technique perfected by him. The technique is best worked on prepared vellum backed for stability. She has to work very quickly to achieve the flat colour background, and to do this it is best to have two brushes fully loaded to the correct consistency. Having outlined the image, a loose wash is rapidly swept over the entire background area, and while still wet a second layer of paint, slightly stiffer, is laid over it. The two layers 'bleed' into each other to dry flat. She now aims to follow Hilliard's method of painting with real gold and silver.

In contemporary portraiture she uses the stipple technique, completing the background before concentrating on facial details. In still life or portraiture, she looks for contrasts of colour and surface textures and likes to include reflective metals and glass in still life paintings whenever possible.

Having completed the outline of a work on tracing paper, she uses a light box to transfer the image on to the ivorine. For painting she works at a sloping desk. Her colours include ultramarine, cobalt blue, cerulean blue, gamboge, vermillion, rose madder, burnt umber, vandyke brown, lamp black and china white: all Winsor and Newton paints. Her brush sizes are 00, 1 and 7 and she emphasizes that as much care is necessary in the framing as in the painting.

Her favourite subjects are portraits, still life and farmyard scenes of rare breeds, and she still paints architectural subjects. Recently she was commissioned to paint a 1927 Bugatti, the pride of the purchaser's vintage car collection.

Elaine greatly admires the Dutch, French and Spanish 17th century masters like Pieter Claesz, Sebastian Stoskopff and Velazquez. The style of that period has particularly influenced her still life compositions. She loves history and the costumes of the 16th and 17th century in portraiture. Elaine is a young artist already held in high esteem and her work is in much demand.

ROBERT HUGHES

by Jo Clay with Elizabeth Johnson

Robert Hughes was born in London in 1934 and lives now in Wiltshire surrounded by the beautiful countryside which inspires many of his landscape paintings. He started painting professionally in 1982 without ever having received any formal art training. His first exhibitions in Marlborough soon gained him a reputation in the art world. Now he also regularly exhibits in London, York, Salisbury and Bath. In 1986 the RMS recognised his ability by awarding him an associate membership (ARMS). His full membership (RMS) was gained in 1989. He has also been a member of the Hilliard Society since 1989.

Robert recently gave up a very successful commercial career to concentrate on his art. He works at home and displays his paintings adjacent to his studio; he also exhibits in galleries in other parts of the country, occasionally undertaking commissions. He is very well-disciplined and sets himself definite targets, which he usually achieves. He admires most of the work of the French Impressionists, and the English painters, especially Constable and Turner. Like many artists, Robert listens to music while painting, which helps him to produce some of the finest miniatures available today. The detail in his paintings is achieved without a magnifying glass. He uses up to twelve brushes of different sizes for each one. His work is mostly oil paint on board, and he varies his techniques to include gouache and watercolour on other surfaces. In addition to landscapes, his subjects include still life and animals.

Robert usually starts painting with the shape and format of the finished work in mind. Presentation is very important, so the frame is always chosen to complement the painting. He pictures the scene in his mind first, and transcribes the image on to prepared board. He also works from photographs occasionally, and carries his camera with him, never missing an opportunity to capture a suitable composition.

The palette he uses is based on eight earth colours, such as yellow ochre and burnt sienna, plus black and white. Once he has painted the main scene he quite often adds figures and animals. Particular satisfaction comes with the knowledge that he has completed an especially good picture and that he knows he can continue to improve and produce even better work. Thinking of an original title can be difficult.

Robert Hughes' paintings are in private collections throughout this country, as well as in the USA, France, Japan, Australia and New Zealand. The author has often admired them in the Medici Gallery in London and at the Hilliard Society exhibitions.

CDR. G. W. G. HUNT RN

During the 1939 War, the incident of watching a sailor disentangle a landmine from a telegraph pole decided the young Geoff Hunt on a career in the Royal Navy. He joined up at the age of 16 as a Cadet at the Royal Naval College at Dartmouth in 1949. Later he trained at sea in the vintage cruiser *HMS Devonshire*, the aircraft carrier *Theseus*, and the corvette *Leeds Castle*.

While ashore at the Royal Naval College, Greenwich, he took the opportunity to study modern art for a while at Goldsmiths' College before returning to sea as a seaman officer in small ships. There followed an interesting and varied career involving travel abroad as well as service ashore and afloat. After leaving the Navy in 1988, two and a half years as Superintendent of the Hong Kong Sea School followed, before he returned home to devote more time to his painting.

With his experience of the sea, who could have better knowledge of its moods and dangers? So it is natural that the subjects of his miniature paintings, mainly seascapes, have earned him an ARMS.

He started miniature painting when his wife, who collects antique snuff boxes, asked him to decorate the lid of a plain one. He did a 'lunchtime sketch' of St James' Park and carried out the work in oils. In retrospect, he says it was 'crude', but a number of commissions resulted. He changed to acrylics, which enabled him to continue his painting while on his travels. Also he decided that concentrating on miniatures would enable him to carry his materials more easily.

Now he works exclusively in acrylics, either on antique boxes or small panels, with Rowley paints and Chinese brushes. In Hong Kong these brushes are remarkably inexpensive so he returned to Britain with a hundred in a box, and they retain their points fairly well. He usually finishes off with two or more coats of varnish but occasionally, when he wants a mellow effect and a robust surface for a 'working' box, it is finished with copal varnish.

Normally he does a few quick pencil sketches first; an essential stage for the more complex battle pictures is to ensure that the perspective is correct. He does a colour/tone sketch in acrylic on paper before beginning the painting itself, after priming the surface with acrylic Gesso primer. He virtually removes the 'tooth' with a very fine abrasive.

Next, the entire picture is painted with a light wash, which is much the same as the earlier colour sketch. The next stage is to do the sky and the sea, with the distant objects, before starting on the main features, the ships and warships. He builds up gradually with a considerable amount of overpainting. Finally, he finishes the highlights on the sea in the foreground, which are the bow wave, the wake and the foam and so on.

He puts much effort into research, be it battle or old ship, and usually provides a 'potted history' with the painting. Although he uses contemporary paintings, prints and photographs for details, he reconstructs the battle scenes essentially from the texts and contemporary maps. He possesses much resource material of his own: books, flags, rigging and so forth, but when necessary he uses the National Maritime Museum Library and photographic archives.

Three of his miniature paintings, acrylic on board, in the 1990 RMS Exhibition, reflected the fascination he has for the subjects. However, he also paints birds, flowers, animals and the occasional vintage car or aircraft. 'Artistic licence,' he claims, 'is an essential ingredient of art, but it must be eschewed when it comes to recording historical events and matching the set of the sail with the wind, or the wind with the sea'.

The resulting authenticity and accurate detail enhances his artistry, appealing as much to the yachtsman as to the collector. Much of his work is painted on commission, but he also exhibits in a number of London galleries as well as with the Hilliard Society and RMS.

JOAN JOYCE

Joan Joyce chose her career in Art at the age of four, as most of her family were involved with arts and crafts. However, owing to the War, she was unable to take an Art training but was 'thrust' into secretarial work in her late 'teens. She also studied Antiques and Photography. On marriage in 1964 she revived her interest in painting and attended Harrow College of Art and Technology for a five-year course. Committee work for several photographic and art societies led to her being Chairman of Visual Arts on the Harrow Arts Council for nearly six years. She also taught portraiture privately in Pinner.

By 1979 she began to help with tours at the Materials' Factory in Wealdstone for Winsor and Newton, and took over as Tour Guide Administrator in 1987.

In the summer of 1987 she began studying miniature painting at Great Missenden with Elizabeth Davys Wood, PSLm, who ran her own Diploma course which Joan completed successfully. It covered materials, surfaces, oil or water-based paint, colours, tone and composition and the history of miniature painting, with tuition in presentation, public speaking, methods of teaching and the construction of a course. The course was only held once.

Meanwhile, for Joan, sales and commissions are increasing, and she finds that working at Winsor and Newton gives her a broad insight into the vast history of pigments and modern synthetic methods. Using artists' quality of paints is essential for work that is to be sold, as are the best possible materials including presentation and framing.

Joan finds that working on a slightly tilted surface is best for her. Out of the normal colour range she avoids black, except for silhouettes, which are more difficult than they appear to be. A small amount of artists' quality white gouache for final touches is admissible. She works from life, with photographs to assist her, and accepts any challenge. The outlining colour is chosen with care, depending on whether the subject is a portrait or buildings. Skin tones, she says, are 'vital, subtle and tricky,' as are the leaves and petals of flowers.

Now she is building up a sizeable collection of work, and hoping to have a one-artist exhibition; she also aims to add a studio to her home in Pinner. She is currently teaching Miniature Painting where she began, at Missenden Abbey, Great Missenden.

MEG KINGSTON

It is important to realise the role that patience, as well as skill and artistic sensibility, plays in the creation of a miniature painting. The gift can also be discovered and nurtured in those willing to persevere and who have the 'right temperament'. Each year in the catalogue of the RMS exhibition Suzanne Lucas, President of the RMS, has much to say about this. She maintains, rightly, that the 'host of pre-occupations that militates against excellence', has to be counteracted by the miniaturist. 'They are not given to flamboyance; their endowments are acute observation, honesty, an excellent sense of balance and much sheer wonder at the greatness of beauty in small things' . . . 'a tolerance of even a millimetre is hardly permitted. The physical control required to keep absolutely still while at work . . . is very tiring . . . as one realizes . . . the brush strokes may run to half a million in number.'

Meg has the qualities needed. She trained as an actress and worked on stage and in television, before moving to the village of Evershot in Dorset. She has two grown-up sons working in Landscape Architecture and in Ecology. She only began miniature painting in 1987, in Sherborne, in Jo Clay's class at the Arts Association. Her only previous experience of painting was for A-level Art at school, and more recently her own experimenting with paint on glass.

Once she discovered miniature painting she became dedicated to it. The subjects she chooses are influenced by the animals she loves and the long country walks she takes in the Dorset countryside. Her preference is for wild life in natural settings or rural cottages such as that of Thomas Hardy. Her painting of this was sold almost the first time she exhibited it in 1990, Hardy's centenary year.

The first time she ventured into exhibiting her miniature paintings was with a few other members of the newly-formed Sherborne Miniature Painting Society, whose President is now Sheila Sanford RI RMS. On that occasion, in 1990, Meg had three paintings accepted at the Hilliard Society of Miniaturists, in Wells. Much encouraged by her success, she sent three miniatures to the RMS in London in November that year, all of which were accepted. One of her delightful butterfly paintings was sold for a good price, as well as the one of (Thomas) 'Hardy's Cottage' in Dorset.

It is a mistake for miniature painters to price their work too low. More than a week's work may be involved; sometimes it may be far longer. Other costs to be covered are the expenses of joining Art societies, the cost of submitting for exhibition and the Society's commission to be paid should the painting sell. So too, of course, is the expense of travelling to deliver and collect the miniatures. Meg paints entirely in watercolour on ivorine, with a fine sense of artistry and meticulous care, something quickly recognized by those who see her work. A recent innovation of hers is to paint landscapes and flowers over which tiny cut-out butterflies hover. It was one of these that sold at the RMS in November. It is always refreshing to see originality within the strict confines of the requirements of the RMS Exhibition.

Meg tends to find the initial decision about her subject is the most difficult, but usually solves it by returning to the countryside or her ever-increasing collection of photographs of such things as tree stumps, grasses and old gates or bits of barbed wire. The first two days are spent in despair that she will never achieve her intention. She loves to study the effect of light and textures, especially fur and feathers. Her next ambition is to try oil paints because of their vibrancy of colour effects.

Whatever she paints she will do it with the intensity and discipline of someone trained in the demanding field of dramatic art, to which she sometimes returns for television productions.

ELISABETH LAKE

Elisabeth Lake studied Art at the West of England College of Art in Bristol. The subjects for which her miniatures are mostly known are 'Interiors', mainly based on her home and its surroundings. Her landscapes and figurative work on a large scale were impressionistic, always in oils, never in watercolours.

In 1980, her spontaneous, watercolour sketches evolved into the more disciplined world of the miniature. She became a Member of the Hilliard Society in 1982, ARMS in 1987 and RMS in 1989. She exhibited at the Royal Academy Summer Exhibition in 1986 and was a prizewinner in the RA annual Christmas Card Competition. In 1988 she won the Ulster Miniature Society Overseas Perpetual Trophy, as well as the 'Best in Exhibition Award'. In Canada's International Miniature Exhibition in 1989 she won First Prize, and exhibits widely throughout North America. She also exhibits regularly at the RWA Autumn Exhibitions and at the Royal Bath and West Show.

Her paintings have a warmth and intimacy that is most appealing and create a record of particular places 'in between', that are simple and quiet and often go unnoticed, such as a 'turn in the stairs' or a glimpse 'through and beyond' with light, atmosphere and depth.

Elisabeth works at one end of a long kitchen table in a 'tumbly', overgrown cottage in a place called Hollow Marsh in Somerset, 'against the wooded hillside of the Mendips,' she says, 'surrounded by the peace of the country sounds'. The cottage is crowded with her artistic and musical family of six, and a large dog. Her other interests are writing, playing the piano and concern about Conservation.

Winsor and Newton's best watercolours and their finest Size 000 sable brushes used on Ivorex, or a similar card, is her choice. Her method is to establish the tone over the entire surface from the beginning, with one colour and then another and so on, ending up with the desired depth of tone in a strangely nondescript hue. At this stage she might add any local colour. Then she leaves it overnight, or a day, and allows the paint time to settle into the paper-based surface. Later she can adjust the light, lifting or depressing it, painting over the whole surface with warm or cool colours according to the requirements. She paints 'very dry', to avoid lifting out previous layers of paint.

She photographs all her work. This is useful not only as a record but often as a reference to study. Her colours and technique are sometimes not unlike Impressionistic pictures. At the 1990 Hilliard Society, one of her paintings was raffled and benefited the Society, a gesture typical of the warm-hearted person she is.

DAPHNE LEE

About twelve years ago, Daphne was demonstrating the painting of eggs for a television programme, 'Houseparty'. After that, she decided to transfer to using a more suitable surface. She had been accustomed to doing 'anything in miniature', as a child and at Art school, and has been designing all her life.

Now she paints almost exclusively in watercolour on ivorine, and in 1984 won the HS 'Best in Exhibition' Award. Occasionally she does larger paintings in pastel or oil. She paints other subjects mainly according to her commissions which are usually farm scenes, animals like squirrels, pigs or kids, and toys.

Daphne exhibits at the RMS, the Hilliard Society and the Society of Sussex Painters. Most of her output goes to galleries and she works hard to keep her standard up to the best of her ability, since she is a professional artist, even though a self-taught miniaturist.

Her home is a small Victorian terrace cottage in Sussex with her two whippet dogs. She has to work in cramped conditions in a small extension surrounded by teddy bears and toys, which are the models for her miniature paintings.

At present, her obsession is restoring an old house in France. She finds the physical work is a relaxation in comparison with the disciplined posture required for painting miniatures. She also makes furniture, usually from something else that has been discarded by other people. She has a kiln, which she feels she should use more often, for making ceramic models of animals or clowns. Painting white tiles to re-fire for decorating her kitchen in France is another idea of hers.

For painting miniatures, she works on a sloping surface, and as she is using an old Winsor and Newton box of watercolours, it acts as her palette too. Her range of colours is fairly restricted because she regards only the 'permanent' colours as satisfactory, sometimes with black and white, depending on the subject. She draws her subject before transferring it to the ivorine by using lights underneath it.

The author has bought a number of delightful small greetings cards by Daphne of farmyard animals from the newly-constructed Gallery, the Old School House, Woolland, not far from Blandford, which is exhibiting a few original miniatures. Daphne's miniatures, with her excellent technique and her chosen subjects, are certainly of universal appeal.

SUZANNE LUCAS

Since 1980 Suzanne Lucas has been internationally known as the first woman President of the Royal Society of Miniature Painters, Sculptors and Gravers, (and is most emphatic about its right to the full title, except when abbreviated to RMS). She is also Founder and President of the Society of Botanical Artists. The official inauguration, on 2nd April 1986, was by Professor W. G. Chaloner PhD BSc FRS, at that time President of the Linnean Society of London and an Honorary Member of the SBA. The Society of Botanical Artists is distinguished by being the first and only one in the world and the artists are selected on both their botanical and artistic ability. She is also known as the generous benefactor of two important awards in the Hilliard Society: the 'Best in Exhibition' and 'Best Novice'.

Suzanne Lucas has exhibited at the Royal Academy, the RI, the Paris Salon, in Antwerp and in The Miniature Art Society of Florida. She exhibits regularly with the RMS, apart from exhibitions held in various places such as Liberty's Exhibition Hall, The Mall Galleries and many others. Among the honours and awards she has won during the last eighteen years she has been awarded thirteen Gold Medals for her special studies of toadstools.

She has enjoyed an active, interesting and unusual life, travelling extensively, while also nurturing a fascinating range of interests. These vary from opera and ballet to travel, mountains and deserts, aviation, and the cultivation and collection of plants. The greatest of these, surely, must be her exquisite study of toadstools.

However, she gives the accolade and responsibility for her own success and dedication to perpetual striving for perfection, to her mother, Lydia Craven (Winifred Beeby, RMS), who died in 1985 at the age of ninety-six, still a Member. It was in her loving honour that Suzanne Lucas donated the Gold Memorial Bowl on the ninetieth anniversary of the foundation of the RMS, which coincided with the thirtieth anniversary of her own Membership. She has been President since 1980.

Born in India, where the sounds and colours made a deep impression on her, she was painting at six years old. By twelve, her future absorbing interest in individual flowers was established. Her education at Roedean was followed by studying at Edinburgh, Munich and Grenoble universities. She also became an accomplished linguist. During the war years this ability proved invaluable to her husband's work, as well as her own, in the Free French and British forces, in which they were involved.

At the beginning of the War she had married Pierre Marie Louis Lucas who was afterwards in command of the Free French Units in Egypt. He was the first in the Suez Canal Zone to rally to General de Gaulle. He was promoted to Admiral in the French Navy, 'Chef du Transit de la Compagnie du Canal de Suez'. For services to the Allies he received the decorations of Commandeur de la Legion d'Honneur, Commander of the British Empire and Commandeur de la Marine. In Egypt Suzanne helped with his secret information work and with organising the Forces' Welfare Work. Then, back in England in 1944, her husband joined the Headquarters of General de Gaulle. By 1945 she set off through Paris to Brest, where he was the Military Governor. Despite the recent occupation of Paris at that time, the artistic life of the community was thriving.

She began miniature painting on ivory in Egypt and from then on it flourished. In 1974 an amethystine blue toadstool inspired her to look intently at toadstools and this developed into an extensive study of them.

In her paintings the depth and brilliance of colour is achieved by glazing superimposed layers. She says this technique is equivalent to doing five or six or more paintings on one picture. The composition, often based on the triangle, comes instinctively. One particular colour, she finds, is often present in the whole plant. For example, the purple in the petals may be used to soften or darken the green leaves. White is used only where there is a bloom of white on the plant; grey is avoided, to keep colours clear and vivid. To date, Suzanne Lucas has been painting on ivory, vellum, ivorine or fine paper, and works only from the subject, never relying on photographs.

There is no doubt that Suzanne Lucas is not only an extraordinarily interesting person to meet, but is continuing to render remarkable service in the particular world of art for which she works so tirelessly.

LANDSCAPES ANIMALS BIRDS WATERCOLOUR ON PAPER

ERIC J. MORTON

Accomplished artists who have painted pictures of an average size for many years, sometimes discover the fascination of painting miniatures. This was the experience of watercolourist, Eric Morton, who taught himself the art of miniature painting on acid-free paper about four years ago.

His subjects include landscape, architecture, birds, animals, flowers and butterflies. His birds and animals are all native species, usually adapted from photographs taken by him. He also has other reference material, such as photographs borrowed from friends.

His miniatures are exhibited at the Medici Gallery and Llewellyn Alexander (Fine Paintings) Ltd., opposite the 'Old Vic' Theatre, near Waterloo Station, London.

He delights in watching a picture being gradually built up from the first colour wash to the finished painting, with all its depth of colour. He feels a great sense of achievement, and finds capturing the sunlight and shadow in his paintings is especially rewarding. He was a draughtsman by profession, which is probably why he is attracted by the details of his subject. All natural things hold a fascination for him, but he is not averse to painting mechanical subjects, such as steam locomotives and traction engines, mostly of a bygone era. While painting he enjoys listening to classical music.

He works on a slightly sloping surface, using a stretched paper which prevents cockling. Apart from the normal range of colours, he occasionally chooses a blue-black, mostly for the eyes of animals. The highlight of the eye is usually the white paper left untouched, but sometimes it is modified with a 'bleed-proof' white. This is an American product obtainable in 1 fl. oz. jars, manufactured by Sallis International, Hollywood, Florida, and sold under the name 'Dr P. H. Martin's Bleedproof White'. If applied over any colour the underlying colour will not 'bleed' through it. Blacks are normally made by mixing blues and browns to give the desired effect. Pure tube black is too dominant for anything except eyes.

First he outlines the painting with very pale raw umber. This is followed by blocking in the colours of the subject within those areas with an appropriate very pale basic wash. The painting is gradually worked up with stippling and short strokes until the desired effect is achieved. He usually uses a minute amount of gum arabic with the colours and a hint of cobalt blue for shadow areas.

The brushes he prefers are Winsor and Newton's Series 12 Miniature Sable, in sizes from 1 to 000. The Schoellershammeer Acid Free Paper on which he paints all his miniatures has an extremely fine surface that allows paint to be lifted when necessary.

He cuts his own mounts from conservation mount board, acid free. Eric holds the view that a purchaser has the right to expect a work of value to last a lifetime without yellowing or staining. He also mitres his own frames before their final assembly.

W. P. MUNDY

by Jo Clay and W. P. Mundy

The most prestigious prize in the world for miniature painting is undoubtedly the Gold Memorial Bowl, awarded annually by the President of the RMS. In the second year of its inception, Suzanne Lucas PRMS presented the 18-carat solid gold bowl (said to be worth £20,000) to Bill Mundy. The Society honoured the artist for his portrait of the Queen's Bargemaster, Mr Edwin Hunt. The RMS actually retains the bowl; however, the artist is given a valuable solid silver-gilt replica.

Mr Edwin Hunt is shown resplendent in a red uniform, unchanged in appearance since the times when the monarch travelled by water, and when only the Royal Bargemaster was officially allowed to touch the Royal Personage! These days, among other duties, the Bargemaster rides behind the Monarch on her way to open Parliament and is responsible for the safekeeping of the crown at that time. On the miniature, the uniform extends to the edge of the frame with a band of lettering surrounding the head at the top of the oval, creating the illusion that Edwin Hunt is emerging from the background.

The medals and crown provide more decoration and are faultlessly rendered, as one would expect of an artist of this calibre. Bill Mundy met the Bargemaster when he was in charge of the Watermen at the opening by Queen Elizabeth II of the new Henley Royal Regatta Headquarters.

The portrait was subsequently purchased by Richard Allen, Sotheby's Miniature expert, for a private collector who donated it to the Cincinatti Museum of Art in the USA. One of the judges at the RMS Exhibition at that time, was Mr John Murdoch from the Victoria and Albert Museum, who said he would have been proud to have it for the permanent collection of the V and A.

In the event, a portrait of David Money-Coutts, Chairman of Coutts Bank in London, was presented to the V and A. This portrait was shown at the 1987 Royal Academy Summer Exhibition. It is painted with an ultramarine blue background and includes 16th century style gold lettering which acts as a perfect foil to Mr Money-Coutt's traditional black frock-coat.

In that same year Bill Mundy was the first winner of the Bell Award for the Best Portrait in the Hilliard Society Exhibition. This portrait is of an old character called 'Red Hesser', whom the artist met while on an extended visit to Texas in the USA.

Bill Mundy is regarded as one of the finest portrait miniaturists in the world today. His subjects come from every walk of life and nationality, and include HRH The Duke of Edinburgh, completed after the sitting with Prince Philip at Buckingham Palace, for a larger portrait. Other portraits are of the King of Thailand, the Sultan of Johor (previously Johore) in Malaysia, Quaboos Din Said – the Sultan of Oman, Spike Milligan, Katie Boyle and several Generals.

He has also painted many members of the Johor Royal Family, including the Yang di Pertuan Agong (King) of Malaysia and his Queen (see illustration). In fact, his first painting ever to be accepted at the Royal Academy (in 1977) was of HRH The Sultan of Johore.

In 1989 he presented the portrait of HM King Bhumibol Adulyadej to HRH Princess Maha Chakri Sirindhorn, and in 1990 presented two miniatures of Princess Sirindhorn to Her Royal Highness at Chitralada Palace in Bangkok.

Two miniature portraits were painted of The Duke of Edinburgh. One is in the Royal collection. The other was, with permission, donated to the Grand Order of Water Rats' Charity and was auctioned for over £2,000.

The 1980 *Leisure Painter* published an article by the artist in which he describes in detail his methods of painting a miniature portrait. His technique has been compared to the artist Seurat's Pointillist style, which was perfected at the end of the 19th century, in which individual colours are painted as dots or lines, utilising the ability of the eye to mix them while viewing the painting. Bill Mundy's style is, of course, greatly reduced in size. Using the unmixed colour results in a cleaner unmuddied appearance. Experience dictates the correct strength of each colour. A miniature portrait should have a jewel-like appearance which is a joy when held in the hand, as well as being a portrait in its own right.

Bill Mundy paints approximately twenty to twenty-five miniatures each year and uses both a magnifying glass with built-in daylight bulbs and special magnifying spectacles. He enjoys locating a 'character' and revels in painting lined, elderly men, such as 'Red Hesser'; or even traditional drawn lines on a Maori's face, which he saw and captured in miniature, at the 1990 Henley Regatta. He also favours military subjects, mainly because of the uniforms and the opportunity to paint the medals and orders in exquisite and minute detail.

Although he feels the standard Kolinsky sable brushes have declined in recent years, he keeps scores of brushes in a variety of sizes and shapes at hand. When a brush begins to wear out, usually before the end of a portrait, he finds the blunt point is useful for stippling backgrounds.

Among the illustrations is a 'staged' portrait of jockey James Carter. He reiterates Nicholas Hilliard's advice in his Treatise that absolute cleanliness is vital. In watercolour, mistakes cannot easily be rectified as they can when using gouache or oil as a medium.

Initially, this artist's method of working is to make a very fine pencil drawing, scaled-down in size to fit the oval. After it is traced on to the ivory or vellum a perfect outline is made in yellow ochre for the face and, usually, in Davy's grey for the body. The pencil marks are removed before beginning the painting.

Recently, he finds that painting the clothes first, then the background, before completing the face allows the correct tone to fall into place. His choice of colours for basic flesh tints are yellow-ochre and vermillian with alizarin crimson for highlights and cheeks. A warm sepia gives the deeper shadows at the hair line and around the eyes and nostrils. His favourite touches are adding violet and olive green in unexpected places on the face. Black is only used for the pupil of the eye. For really dark areas, a mixture of sepia and ultramarine (or violet) is preferred. A dot of Chinese white emphasises the highlight of the eye. He believes the directions of the brush strokes must follow the lines and style of the hair.

He takes between thirty and fifty hours to complete a miniature portrait. The important task of selecting the right framing and presentation then follows and, finally, the painting is likely to be placed in a leather and velvet silk-lined case.

Although Bill Mundy specialises in miniature portraits, his larger portraits in watercolour and oils, as well as the *trompe l'oeil* watercolours, attract much attention. He has twice won the 'Exhibit of the Year' award at the Royal Academy Summer Exhibition.

BUILDINGS FLOWERS WATERCOLOUR AND GOUACHE ON WHITE CARD

MAUREEN PEARSON

Although Maureen later elected to enter the more secure medical world, she began 'painting seriously' at the age of eleven. While qualifying in her chosen career, one of her tutors, a refugee from Budapest (to whom she is perpetually grateful), spent many hours passing on to her all the finer points of painting and drawing, brushwork, analysis of light and shade, perspective and composition.

After qualifying, she worked for ten hectic years in her chosen career, combining that with marriage and bringing up her family. She was therefore prevented from having time for painting, but in 1970 she was able to resume it seriously. She then realised that the finely detailed part of her larger pictures appealed to her most. Her first visit to the Hilliard Society Exhibition converted her to miniature painting entirely. From her previous knowledge, and by trial and error, she was able to teach herself the art.

With her first experience of submitting work for exhibition, she found the courage to send three miniatures to the 1990 HS Exhibition in the Bishop's Palace, in Wells. To her surprise she won the award for the 'Best in Exhibition' for her painting 'Woburn Walk in the Rain', in watercolour and gouache on white card. She almost rejected it twice herself previously, but returned to work on it, obviously with great success.

This experience gave her the confidence to submit five works for the November RMS Exhibition in London later that year. All were accepted, and a great sense of achievement followed. She has produced copies for this book of her paintings 'Woburn Walk in the Rain' and 'Black Iris (Swahili)'; both were sold at the RMS Exhibition.

There is much controversy about the ethics of copying paintings. This is acceptable for miniature painting, since it was traditional for early travellers to carry miniature copies of favourite paintings and masterpieces. Maureen acknowledges the value of copying, for learning about the techniques, but has reservations about submitting work for exhibitions that is not original. She herself feels that each new painting is linked in some way to her last one, either in the amount of detail or perhaps in the inclusion of water. However, she prefers the challenge of a difficult subject, as opposed to repetitive studies of one contemplative study.

Because of the long hours involved in painting miniatures, a comfortable sitting position is vital. She sits on an upright Parker Knoll, with a cantilever, adjustable table in front of her, which has a quarter of its surface remaining flat to hold her palette, brushes and water. As a right-handed person, she arranges for the light to come from the left, and finds peace of mind without distraction is essential. For her, the choice of subject is critical. The confidence to execute it must exist. Sometimes she may observe and plan a difficult picture for as long as a month, while working on another.

She uses Winsor and Newton's Artists' Watercolours and also their Designer Gouache, painted on card. A sectioned china (porcelain) palette serves for mixing the paints. One problem, familiar to other miniaturists, is the choice of a suitable brush. However, she has been delighted to discover the Japanese 'Inscribe' brush, Series 2000, No 00000, and another which is Winsor and Newton Series 29, No 00000. It gives her a firmer stroke and is called a 'Spotting Sable'. Her range of colours, apart from the normal ones, include Permanent White and the 'warmer' white, Chinese White. Oxide of Chromium (green) is another.

In her architectural pictures, composition, accurate detail, correct perspective and a sense of depth are imperative. All must be right from the start or the picture is doomed. Once the composition is planned, she removes the pencil guide lines (eye-level lines and reducing lines), leaving only the faint lines of the picture. Next, she paints a single wash of Designer's Gouache Permanent White over the whole area. The fine pencil lines are still visible. Maureen finds the white base offers an easier management of the colours painted on top. If a colour needs to be lightened, or a detail reduced in size, she recommends holding the picture upside down until the colours become bands of colour and more easily identifiable.

The light pathway, she suggests, will often take the viewer past the closest buildings, through to the picture's most distant detail. She advises leaving the light pathway untouched until the last moment. With the gouache base, it may not be necessary to add more than the slightest strokes, bordering a darker colour. It is important to remember that it is rare for a building to look exactly the same colour as the material from which it is made. Whole areas of shadow or reflected sunlight will alter the colours. She often tackles some particularly troublesome detail first, in case it proves too difficult.

Maureen believes that a picture will benefit from a small detail or 'precious' colour (her own word) placed with discrimination, possibly in the middle third of the space available, never the exact centre. This, it seems, is similar to the focal point of a painting. With experience, she is finding that the proportion of successful pictures is increasing. It is a most rewarding hobby and one that she is looking forward to in retirement, with ever-increasing success, among the many beautiful buildings in Bath where she lives.

MICHAEL PIERCE

Watching Michael Pierce demonstrating, in front of a large audience, the art of creating a life-size drawing for a silhouette, is a fascinating experience. He adopted the same method as profilists used in the 18th century. First he asked for a volunteer and then proceeded to strap her arms and body onto a rigid upright chair to render her immobile. For her comfort he did not strap her neck to it, as was traditional in making silhouettes.

So as to obtain a shadow of the profile on a screen and paper for the artist to trace, a candle was placed in front of the sitter, making the profile clearly visible from the other side. One minute was the usual time taken for that to be done. Mike did it to the second and then released his subject. Two hundred years ago, the drawing would have been reduced in size, using an instrument called a pantograph. The smaller version would be painted within the outline, and the finished silhouette would be ready for the purchaser.

In our demonstration, Mike invited a member of the audience (whom he knew were all artists) to cut out his drawing. That completed, he held the white cut-out paper against black paper, for us to see the success of his achievement.

His performance had the panache of a great, experienced Shakespearean actor. For us, it was an unforgetable presentation of his art, for which he usually paints on card or plaster and always with gouache on an ink base.

With his warm and ebullient personality, Mike also provides an audience with an enthralling account of the 'History of Silhouettes', well-illustrated from his own valuable collection of many past famous silhouettists.

The name 'Silhouette' is derived from Etienne de Silhouette (1709-1769), whose hobby was to cut profiles from black paper. In the hands of skilful artists, it became a fairly inexpensive way of producing a small but accurate likeness. By the 18th century, the practice had become an entertaining pastime in England. Also, such likenesses were less expensive than having conventional portraits painted; that was before photography arrived.

Many great men sat for their profile portraits, and that form of art attracted Royal Patronage of sitters, such as HRH the Prince Regent, later George IV, William IV and Queen Victoria.

It is with this background that Mike developed his art from a very early age and is now recognized nationally and internationally. He was introduced to the profile technique by the late W. Ellis, a tutor at the Slade and a notable Victorian miniaturist.

Today, Mike has developed his art to the point of his being one of the small number of artists dedicated to the preservation of this most painstaking of arts and is the only one in full time practice. Apart from silhouettes of people, animals and objects, he regularly undertakes commissions for invitations, Christmas cards and company logotypes. His work has many other commercial applications, in which his ability to blend past and present becomes uniquely original.

His studio in an arcade opposite the Cathedral in West Street, Chichester is entirely decorated in a style reminiscent of the period he recreates so beautifully, with Georgian-style hand-painted wallpapers. The ceilings are moulded plaster, a canary is in a brass cage and an aspidistra on a lace-covered table. Even the frames he uses are made to his own design and complement the period.

In 1977 he was invited to produce profiles of the Queen and the Duke of Edinburgh for the Silver Jubilee and an exhibition followed in the Goldsmiths' Hall in London. His silhouette miniatures are now collected all over the world. He says he limits himself to 700 a year, so as to avoid becoming 'a sausage machine'.

Mike's greatest achievement, created to commemorate the 50th Anniversary of the Battle of Britain in 1990, as a Commemorative Folio, is the production of a superb book. 401 copies were made and Number 1 was presented to Her Majesty The Queen. Each folio costs £1,600, and up to date Mike has raised between £300,000 and £400,000 for the Royal Air Force Benevolent Fund.

No book, he says, has ever been produced to a higher standard, with special gold-tipped paper and colour plates protected by acid-free tissue. The covers are finished in selected Chieftain goat skins, dyed the exact shade of the RAF wartime uniform, with a gold-blocked cover and a title that incorporates specially woven RAF wings of the 1940 type with the King's Crown. Mike designed the book to pay tribute to the pilots of the wartime Royal Air Force, and he has painted twenty-five silhouettes of a representative few, as they are now; he illustrated it throughout with thumbnail sketches of aircraft or pilots.

Simply by using his imagination, artistic abilities and time for the benefit of others, what better gift could there be to such a worthwhile cause? Their record was made with the help of other gifted men, the well-known photographer, Roy Asser, Bill Gunston, the aviation historian, John Golley, World War II fighter pilot, Ian Dunning, now writing for the *Sunday Times*, and Brian Masterton, a traditional book designer.

Obviously, visiting Chichester is very worthwhile, especially to see this magnificent production and to meet a man of his calibre.

DARTMOOR LANDSCAPE WATERCOLOUR ON BRISTOL BOARD

ROSALIND PIERSON

The Hilliard Society was founded by Rosalind Pierson and Sue Burton at the beginning of 1982 to provide further public knowledge about miniature painting and to put patrons and collectors in touch with the artists, amongst its other aims. The name of Hilliard was adopted because the Society is in the South West, and Nicholas Hilliard, born in Exeter in 1547, was one of the first great miniaturists. The annual Spring exhibition of the Society is held in the Bishop's Palace in the Cathedral City of Wells.

At many of the exhibitions to which she submits work, clusters of people armed with magnifying glasses gather round paintings with a red dot, signifying they are Rosalind's miniatures. The perfection of her art is evident. Her subjects are scenes of the Dartmoor and Devon countryside, with its undulating hills, stone walls or streams, which are familiar to those who see her work regularly. They satisfy the wishes of conservationists. Sheep graze quietly in the unspoilt landscape, as far as the eye can see, or rustling rock-filled brooks sparkle with light under the tracery of overhead branches. All her watercolours are encapsulated on Bristol board in an area the size of a playing card. The light and colour are scintillating.

Meeting her is little clue to her 'secret art'. She hides her shyness with a charming smile. Her intensity of effort seems to be carried weightlessly by her seemingly relaxed disposition. The 'joie de vivre' she feels for nature is expressed entirely in her paintings. Her perfectionist technique does the rest.

She received her art training at the Ruskin School of Drawing and Fine Art, which gave her the breadth and depth of an artistic background many of us might envy. Her first work was accepted at the Royal Academy. It seems that nothing but success followed, with annual exhibitions at Tavistock, where her home is. Further work was accepted at the Academy, the RMS and, in 1979, the Paris Salon. In 1977 she became ARMS, and in 1980 a full member of the RMS. In 1978 she was awarded a silver medal at the Paris Salon and accepted as an Associate Member of the Société des Artistes Français. In the centenary year of the 'Société', she was awarded a gold medal at the Salon. She has also exhibited her work with the Bilan de l'Art Contemporain in Paris, Quebec and New York; and at the Medici Gallery, London; Hereford, Yorkshire, Monaco, Florida, Montana, West Virginia and Ulster. Among her various awards, she won the Hilliard Society 'Best in Exhibition' in 1985, the RMS 'Gordon Drummond Award' in 1987 and the Ulster

Overseas Award in 1990. In 1989 at her exhibition in the Tavistock Town Hall there were about 90 paintings; half of them were Dartmoor scenes.

Rosalind works from her own photographs. Her paints and brushes are Winsor and Newton's, Series 12 and 16. Among her colours are three yellows, six greens and four blues. She outlines in faint pencil, rubbing out some of the lines before painting the sky first, using a wash of colour, then a stippling technique for the rest of the picture, keeping the paints fairly dry. Her aim is to be able to paint a 'good cloudy sky' and specialise in Dartmoor landscapes which few people can capture. She wants to be one of the few.

JOYCE ROGERSON

The miniatures in the Victoria and Albert Museum in London were the especial inspiration for turning Joyce towards miniature painting. She always painted in great detail, having started as a child, largely because her mother was also painting and drawing.

In 1983 she began painting miniatures, mainly watercolour landscapes and still-life, though birds and aspects of nature are her forte. She likes watercolour on vellum and Arches HP paper, but mainly uses it on ivorine. She takes on many commissions nationally and internationally and her miniature painting of a swan has been accepted by the Society of Wildlife Art of the Nations. Her aim is to make traditional records of nature, and she claims to have an 'obsession' about birds. She finds there is little time for other activities in her life, but does enjoy ballet.

Joyce says she spends as much time watching birds as painting them. 'It is important to observe their characteristics and keep a mental image of them to record later in drawings or paintings.' Like many artists, she finds walking in the countryside a source of inspiration, especially for background material and the correct habitat for the bird or animal. Most British mammals, being nocturnal, are difficult to find, so it is infinitely easier to paint birds. She visits many nature reserves and sanctuaries. The Weyhill Hawk Conservancy at Andover is ideal for falcons and owls.

She tries to sketch them very quickly and also backs the sketches up with her own photographs. A large collection of stuffed birds and some butterflies, most of which were road casualties, give her additional material for her work. Friends and relations present her with 'unfortunate victims'. After freezing them, she posts them to an excellent taxidermist. She had to turn down one offer of a badger as there was not enough room in the freezer!

The easiest birds to paint are the ones that land in the garden. In Haslemere there is an excellent natural history museum, which is most useful when she is searching for some bird that is not often seen. They have most of the British birds in their collection.

She cuts the ivorine to fit the frame, having washed it with detergent. Next she secures it in a block of polystyrene with pins placed around the ivorine. Having chosen the subject from her hundreds of drawings, she draws it directly on to the ivorine with an automatic pencil, a 0.3 mm Pentel. Then she removes any excess lead with a kneadable rubber, so that just a faint outline remains. Then she is ready for painting. Joyce prefers pans to tubes of paint as they do not contain so much glycerine.

She finds they become too sticky on ivorine. Her range of colours is a normal one, with white gouache as well. She uses both Rowney and Winsor and Newton paints, while her brushes are series 7 and 12, sizes 000, 00, 0, 1, 2 and 4.

When she starts painting, the washes are very fine. She then builds up the picture with stippling and hatching and, finally, uses white mixed with another colour, such as yellow ochre for highlights and the highlight of the eye.

The delicacy of her handling of the paints ensures that her miniature paintings are much sought after in the exhibitions. In March 1991 she has been 'Highly Commended' for the 'Ulster Savings Perpetual Trophy 1991' at the Ulster Society of Miniaturists.

FLOWERS PORTRAITS LANDSCAPES ANIMALS WATERCOLOUR OILS PASTELS

MARGARET RYDER

In the original planning of this book each artist was listed under one main category by which the artist, it seemed, was most widely known. Margaret Ryder came under the title 'Flowers', until she, like many others, requested to be classified under at least three of the subjects they painted as miniatures. 'I painted my first portrait sixty-two years ago,' she wrote, and she has painted portraits, as well as wild life, flowers and animals, ever since. The author has enjoyed a lively correspondence with Margaret, who claims she is 'not at all an interesting person,' which of course is not at all true.

She is a versatile artist and as such is a valued member of the RMS (as one of the three Vice-Presidents) and of the Hilliard Society. She paints in a very distinctive style with strong contrasting tones and colours. The medium may be watercolour on ivory for portraits, or in watercolour, oils or pastel on vellum for other subjects.

In 1987 she was awarded an 'Honourable Mention' for the RMS 'Gold Memorial Bowl Award'. She has exhibited at the Royal Academy, the Paris Salon, the Pastel Society, the Royal Institute, the Manchester Academy, with the Aberdeen Society of Artists, in Perth, Australia, and Pittsburg in the USA, as well as having had five one-artist shows and four joint shows with a fellow artist. She has written an informative feature in the *Leisure Painter* about her methods; and has given talks about the History of Miniature Painting. She is certainly a remarkable person.

She was born Margaret Elaine Wordsworth in 1908, and believes she is distantly related to the poet but was glad to change her name on marriage to N. V. Ryder. He is now a remarkable 87-year-old, but at that time she was glad to change her name to a shorter one. ('Easier to sign on miniatures' she says!) Her training began in Sheffield, where she still lives. At the Sheffield College of Art she won numerous scholarships, before working for three years in commercial art in London and Manchester. After her two children, Peter and Angela, were born, she worked for twenty-five years as a freelance artist.

She is a member of the National Council of Women, a Soroptimist and President of The Sheffield Society of Women Artists which holds a successful exhibition annually and meets monthly for lively interchanges and for viewing each others' current work. When she comes to London to take an active part in organising the RMS Exhibition, she is able to stay with her daughter, a former Bluebell Girl.

She has a compact studio built on to the back of their house overlooking the garden, warm and comfortable for her sitters. Margaret insists she is 'a fairly ordinary person' as she spends most of her time working. Nevertheless, she has time to enjoy music and 'all creatures great and small', (except spiders).

In her feature in the June 1986 *Leisure Painter,* she outlines the origins of miniature painting and gives an explanation of specific terms. Then a brief survey of the History of Miniature Painting preceded the account of her own painting methods, starting with the advice to stick the ivory or vellum on to a larger card to avoid handling marks. A small amount of pumice powder sprinkled on to the surface and rubbed with the palm of the hand, assures that the surface is free of grease.

For portraits she chooses the 'tried and true colours', sepia, raw and burnt sienna, raw and burnt umber, cobalt, crimson and scarlet lake, light red and Paynes grey, preferring tubes, to keep the paint fresher. She needs a large selection of colours for flowers and suggests the artists' colour chart should be checked for the permanence of each colour.

For portraits, she makes drawings to enable the sitter to relax before she takes photographs to cut down the sitting time. Her drawing for the portrait is transferred to the ivory with a weak solution of cobalt and burnt sienna, very faintly. She does not use washes except for the background, and works with an 0 brush, either by cross-hatching or shading with gum water as a medium. For this she dissolves a small amount of gum arabic in boiling water and keeps it corked in a container. The next stage is to work up the portrait, checking with a magnifying glass to detect errors. When painting flowers on vellum with a fairly dry brush, she starts with one flower and then searches for others to fit around it. She often 'vignettes' round the edge of the vellum, starting faintly and deepening the colour towards the frame.

Meeting Margaret is like encountering a warm-hearted old friend, and these qualities have much to do with miniature painting.

LANDSCAPES WATERCOLOUR ON ARCHES PAPER OR VELLUM

SHEILA SANFORD

Sheila Sanford was born in Singapore and came to England with her younger sister when they were aged six and seven, to boarding school. It was there she discovered her talent for drawing and painting; in fact it was the only subject which came easily to her.

During the war she joined the WRNS and after a few months found her niche in the Drawing Office painting diagrams of gun emplacements and shells - not exactly an artistic achievement, but a start.

After the war the government of the day gave grants to all ex-Service men and women and Sheila elected to take a course in Fine Art at St Martin's School of Art in London, where she met her husband Roy, a graphic artist. They then worked together doing finished artwork for advertising and publishing, Sheila painting book jackets and magazine illustrations whilst Roy (Letraset being non-existent then) hand-lettered the type.

After having twins, and five years later another baby, she gave up painting for five years in order to look after the family. It was very difficult breaking into the commercial world again after such a long absence, so she painted just for pleasure.

In 1970 Sheila and her family moved to Shaftesbury, in Dorset, where they opened a gallery in their home and exhibited the works of well-known artists and potters. Although the Gallery was very enjoyable and more or less self-sustaining, there was not much time left for painting; so in 1980 they moved to South Dorset, to a village near Bridport. Meanwhile their friends in Gillingham, printers Rob and Sue Neely, had bought a new Heidelburg colour lithograph machine, which they wanted to try out using detailed paintings. They asked Sheila to lend them some miniatures to experiment with, and having produced some excellent prints, decided they had better 'set to' and sell them. This was the beginning of a very successful enterprise and the firm *Skittle Prints* is now well established.

In the late Seventies, Sheila found parts of the detail of her larger work took too long to complete. As a result, in a conversation with her framer, he suggested that she should use the spare pieces of card he normally threw away as mounts for miniatures. This is how Sheila Sanford became a watercolour miniaturist.

She exhibited at the RMS and later was made a Full Member. She also exhibits annually at the Miniature Art Society of Florida, where she has won numerous awards. In 1990, she won the 'Excellence in all Entries' Award, and First in 'Landscape'.

She is also a member of the Royal Institute of Painters in Watercolours, where she shows larger paintings, but she prefers the discipline of miniature work. She now works entirely in watercolour and her later work is executed on vellum, a medium she finds very sympathetic to her style of painting.

She is well-known throughout Dorset for her delightful paintings of the Dorset countryside and cottages and particularly for her miniatures, which are reproduced as greetings cards. The author enjoyed her most successful exhibition, which was held in conjunction with Sir Hugh Casson, in 1989 in the Alpha Gallery in East Coker, near Yeovil. Sheila is certainly an extremely successful artist, and her husband Roy is a most supportive partner as a Director in their business.

ILLUMINATIONS WATERCOLOUR ON VELLUM AND IVORINE

HENRY SAXON

Henry Saxon was introduced to miniature painting by the late John Spenser (Hon.RMS), at Chesterfield in about 1956. His instruction was invaluable. However, Henry did not take it seriously until later. He had a basic art training as a full-time student at Manchester School of Art, followed by several years of designing for commercial printing, including an introduction to illuminating (as on the old manuscripts). Finally he became Studio Manager in Litho Reproduction.

His favourite medium is in watercolour for miniatures. He uses ivory rarely, the surface is mainly vellum on Bristol board, which is the material for his illustrated scripts. They are uniquely beautiful and won for him, among other awards, the Hilliard Society 'Best in Exhibition' in 1986, the RMS Gold Bowl in 1989 and in the UMS he won the 'Madam MacCarthy Mór Memorial Bowl 1990' and the 'Ulster Savings Perpetual Trophy 1991', for one miniature, and Highly Commended for another, for the same award.

His own style of work emanates from original illuminations. When illuminating, he does the main text, followed by any raised preparation and then the application of gold leaf and burnishing, colour work, capitals and finally the illustration, using a handrest for all these operations. Thus the small illustrations within an illuminated text are produced last, on the carefully prepared surface.

After completing the calligraphy and designs for the illustrated scripts of poems, passages of scripture and other texts, he adds the minute, raised landscapes and still life watercolour pictures. These he paints separately on ivorine. One example is the raised 'Windsor Castle' that is part of the illumination 'I Vow to Thee my Country'. Henry describes the process as 'bonding a piece of ivorine of about one inch by half an inch (with the edges shaved all round) to the decorated vellum'. The effect of these faultlessly executed texts is exquisite. Most people have never seen such perfect caligraphy on such a small scale. However, more recently, other miniaturists are taking up the challenge to see if they can compete.

When painting his miniatures he prefers to work on a slightly sloping surface. He uses mainly Winsor and Newton colours. If he is reducing large drawings to a smaller size he draws a graph, and so reduces it to a smaller size with a two-line proportional system.

Now that he has retired (and is working harder than ever), he has time to look at more manuscripts and illuminations, wherever he can find them. He does not seek any particular market, but works on commission and exhibits them at the RMS, HS and UMS. He claims to be somewhat lazy by nature and enjoys the outdoor life. So he paints, when possible, from 6 am; and being a 'do-it-yourself' man, then works on his car and house, at woodwork, photography or in his garden. He also enjoys sport, fishing and walking. 'Not a social man,' he says; and seems anything but lazy. He gives occasional demonstrations and sometimes takes sketching parties. Above all, he is extremely modest about his commendable achievements, which earn great admiration for his work.

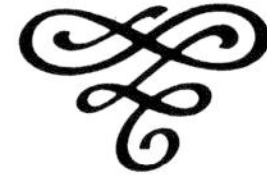

SYDNEY SHORTHOUSE

In the 1988 Hilliard Society Newsletter, Sydney Shorthouse wrote a feature about his portrait of Harold Larwood, the famous Nottinghamshire county cricketer, the Club's most famous player. It raised £2,000 by being auctioned in aid of the Club's new stand and also facilities intended for the development of cricket for young people at Trent Bridge, Nottingham. The event was televised live by BBC2. Such publicity inevitably promotes the career of an artist, but by that time Sydney was already becoming known as an extremely good miniature portraitist and commissions were coming in consistently.

The awards he wins provide sufficient evidence of his present reputation, beginning with the Hilliard Society 'Best Novice Award' (shared) in 1985. In 1989 in the Miniature Painters, Sculptures and Gravers' Society of Washington, DC, he won first place in the International Section, and in 1990 an 'Honourable Mention' in the Lavinia White Boardman Memorial Award (for painting) on Ivory and Ivorine; and also in 1990, in the Miniature Art Society of Florida, he won second place in the 'Portrait Award'.

In his early life he was much influenced by his mother who was a very creative person with considerable ingenuity for making things from odds and ends. Sydney thought all children had this experience with one or other parent and only later realised how lucky he was. Also in his background is the memory of being captivated by the deft sketching of a maternal uncle. Interest heightened when he was given a box of Winsor and Newton watercolours at a Sunday School sports day at the age of eight. Since that time he began putting images from the countryside on to paper. When he was eleven years old he came under the influence of an Art master who illustrated his own books on ornithology with pen and ink washes. So Sydney found himself using fine pens and was intrigued by the innumerable dots in black and white press photographs, which he spent hours emulating. Doubtless that was excellent preparation for miniature painting, unbeknown to him. He wishes now he had been introduced to portrait painting in those early years.

Sadly for him, his father did not see Art as a possible career for his son in the 1930s, but wanted a more secure future for him. That was in the offices of the Gas Works; so Sydney lost the opportunity of taking a place in Art School, which resulted in a waning of his interest in Art.

His precious security was shattered with the outbreak of war, when with some relief he joined the RAF. After the war, the chance to use his artistic talents arose in the most unexpected place: the Gas Industry! He became Head, in due course, of the new Design and Production Centre, serving the needs of 112 gas undertakings in the East Midlands for shop designs, displays and exhibitions.

Undoubtedly this experience has helped him launch his retirement career in painting portrait commissions. His first portrait was of his grandson (undertaken with some trepidation) but it led to his first commission. Then the Hilliard Society accepted his work, as did the RMS later. So he recaptured the dream that eluded him in his youth, and he now finds the miniature societies provide a wealth of pleasure through his progressive successes and the friendships he makes.

The procedure he adopts, when painting a portrait, is to outline the subject in ultramarine from the drawing made from the 'grid' he sets up; a technique used by the Old Masters. Three to four hours of work doing this precede the five to six hours in establishing the eyes, brows, nose, mouth and chin and the rest of the facial area. On the second day, four to five hours will be spent on the hair, depending on its simplicity or otherwise. On the third day, three or more hours will be spent on the background. He uses a little oxgall in his paint mixtures on the ivory or ivorine; but never black, and only rarely white for the highlights of eyes or jewellery. The usual range of colours are Winsor and Newton Artists' Quality Watercolour tubes.

During the last few years Sydney has been an excellent correspondent, and in rereading the advice and help he has given the author perhaps his description of the approach to miniature painting has been the best. 'First and foremost,' he wrote, 'miniature painting is about the development of the finest and most demanding of practical skills of all the painting arenas. It is the mastery of the handling of the tiny brush to produce the quality work which still maintains the quality when magnified, say, six times. Stipple, line, hatch work, so fine, that much of the technique is lost to the eye.'

Sydney is not only very dedicated to his work, but is an example to all retired people for launching himself into an absorbing and profitable career so successfully. His son Andrew, already well-established in another career, is following in his father's footsteps. Meanwhile Sydney is held in high esteem by both the Hilliard Society and the RMS.

BARBARA VALENTINE

Since 1984 Barbara Valentine has worked solely in miniatures. Trained at Goldsmiths' College School of Art in Illustration, she was awarded a National Diploma in Design in 1964. When her family was young she worked in various branches of art, all of which provided an excellent basis for miniature painting.

Her friend Joan Batty introduced her to miniatures, and miniaturist Elizabeth Davys Wood (who founded the Society of Limners in May 1986 and taught miniature painting in many adult colleges), further stimulated and helped her. Most of her miniatures are watercolour on ivorine, occasionally oil. For pendants and box lids she sometimes works on vellum. She sells mainly at the Medici Society and exhibitions arranged through Pauline Leck.

Barbara's husband, Louis Dodd, whom she met and married while at art school, is one of the top marine painters in the country. Their two children are also in artistically orientated fields, sculpture and photography.

Barbara admits she could earn more money with larger paintings, but they are not for her. 'People who buy miniatures are very special people,' she maintains. She works in a lovely studio, full of beautiful objects, which 'feels like being in the middle of a still-life.' Because her son is a photographer, she has access to rejected photographs. The shiny back of them acts as a good surface, like a palette, or ivorine on which to experiment with colours and technique. She tends to use Winsor and Newton pans for darker colours and tubes for the lighter ones; and very little white; never black, except for silhouettes, which are purely for demonstration purposes. Her favourite brushes are Da Vinci Needlepoints for fine detail.

She teaches an adult evening class at Claverham Community College and, as with all good teachers, learns much from them too. While working, they often listen to music suitable for the painting session, mostly Bach.

Constantly striving for perfection is essential to her. The next picture is always the best. Her favourite subjects are her versions of wild flowers, influenced by the Dutch masters she so much admires, and still-life pictures. These have intricate meanings expressed in the significance of the objects and their juxtapositions. She believes the study and copying of the early miniatures is the best education possible for this art form.

When painting modern portraits, ideally she likes to talk to the 'subjects', to know what they are really like, before making some colour sketches and then taking photographs (for working by herself), while still retaining the inspiration. She regards parting with her paintings as 'sharing her perceptions of things'.

One particular feature of her personality is her gift for healing. When possible, she talks to her 'patients' and finds out what portrait, place or pet might give them a sense of peace; or they give her something to use as a painting in a pendant which they keep as a talisman. She has had some very good results, thus providing evidence of the soothing effect of a miniature painting. She is one of those people who is concerned about others, the hallmark of a first rate teacher. Her students in East Sussex are most fortunate to have someone who imparts her own knowledge of miniature painting so well.

FLORENCE YOUNG

As a self-taught artist, Florence Young, who began painting in oils in 1967 at the age of thirty-nine, has achieved much. Apart from membership of the RMS and of the Society of Women Artists, she was also a Member of the 'Société des Artistes Français' from 1968-1989, where she gained three major awards, including a silver medal.

Her miniature painting began when a local photographer, who produced the ivory and frame, wanted a miniature painting of his gun dog. The resulting oil painting, she feels now, was a waste of ivory, but it led to three more commissions of dogs. Then she saw an advertisement for the RMS Exhibition, and learned a great deal from 'just looking' and reading the descriptions of the individual miniatures, having had the foresight to take a magnifying glass. After that, she was fortunate in being put in touch with Truda Mordue RMS, for criticism. Since then she has worked hard to achieve her many successes, and is one of those people who experiences joy in the wide variety of subjects she paints, mainly watercolour on vellum, and in oils on hard board.

She is a person of initiative, who grasps any opportunity to portray unusual or historical 'events'. For example, she created a group of miniatures, which are probably unique, of old boats (principally at what was St Katherine's Dock Boat Museum) and of transients in the West India Dock. Those paintings have been exhibited in the Paris Salon, the RMS and SWA. Her aim is to exhibit them as a collection, because the Boat Museum is non-existent now.

On one occasion, while sketching at St Katherine's Dock Boat Museum, she realised she needed one more boat for her RMS grouping. She happened to see a television programme mentioning an expedition to the Antarctic, and found that the boat for transporting the expedition (and to be used as a base), was at the West India Docks by the deserted Canary Wharf. Later, while she was sketching it, a member of the crew came to see her work and managed to 'escort her on board'; (a euphemistic way of avoiding her own words describing her efforts, as a 'geriatric struggling to keep up with him', so that she could check the rigging and other paraphernalia on deck. She refused to part with the resulting miniature, but had it photographed and framed for presentation to the ship, The Southern Quest. The ship was a vital part of the 'Expedition in the Footsteps of Scott', lasting two years. Sadly, the ship was smashed in the ice. As a result of her involvement she was invited to the first lecture by Robert Swan and Roger Mear, given at the Royal Geographical Society. Robert Swan is the only man to have walked to both ends of the earth. Later in the book he brought out, he acknowledged her contribution to recording 'live history'.

A few years ago she began teaching at Fittleworth at the Old Rectory, which is an Adult Residential Centre, near Pulborough. She teaches a 'four days' and a 'seven days' session, on a one-to-one basis in a concentrated course. One essential ingredient is good light, as miniature paintings are usually done indoors. Preliminary sketches, such as of flowers or trees, are encouraged. Her students are expected to have done oil or watercolour painting to a fairly high standard. Also, Florence has tutored H. F. Holidays Ltd (i.e. Holiday Fellowship Holidays) at many centres throughout the country. Her other important work included teaching art for therapy for people who have had mental problems.

She has been invited to exhibit with a wide range of galleries and societies including the Royal Watercolour Society of Flower Painting, the Pastel Society, the Royal Institute of Painters in Watercolour, and has had work accepted for the Royal Academy, among many others. She has also been commissioned for her work from a wide group of businesses or people. She has biographical entries in the Second Edition of the 'International Who's Who in Art and Antiques', 'The World of Women' and 'Who's Who in Art'. She is a lively and enterprising person, who has an excellent rapport with people, apart from being a very successful artist.

LIST OF MINIATURISTS

1 MARGARET ADAMS ARMS HS
2 PHYLLIS ARNOLD RMS PUSM PUSWA SM HS FIBA
3 JENNY BROOKS Dip.AD ATC HS
4 W. M. BURDETT-SOMERS ARMS MAA HS
5 JENNIFER BUXTON RMS HS
6 HEATHER O. CATCHPOLE RMS HS
7 SYLVIA CAVE MA HS
8 LOVEDA COX HS
9 PAMELA DAVIS RMS HS
10 PAULINE DENYER Des.RCA HS SLm
11 PHOEBE SHOLTO DOUGLAS RMS HS
12 SHEILA FAIRMAN RMS FSBA SWA HS
13 ELAINE FELLOWS ARMS SWA HS USM
14 ROBERT HUGHES RMS HS
15 CDR. G. W. G. HUNT RN ARMS HS
16 JOAN JOYCE SLm HS
17 MEG KINGSTON HS
18 ELISABETH LAKE RMS HS
19 DAPHNE LEE RMS HS
20 SUZANNE LUCAS FLS PRMS FPSBA SWA Hon.HS
21 ERIC MORTON ARMS HS
22 W. P. MUNDY RMS HS FSCD
23 MAUREEN PEARSON HS
24 MICHAEL PIERCE SILHOUETTIST AND PROFILIST
25 ROSALIND PIERSON RMS (Co-Founder of THE HILLIARD SOCIETY)
26 JOYCE ROGERSON RMS SWA MASF USM
27 MARGARET RYDER VPRMS SWA FSBA HS
28 SHEILA SANFORD RI RMS
29 HENRY SAXON RMS HS
30 SYDNEY SHORTHOUSE RMS HS
31 BARBARA VALENTINE ARMS SLm HS
32 FLORENCE YOUNG SWA RMS HS

LIST OF ILLUSTRATIONS

Appreciation of the details is enhanced by the use of a magnifying glass.

Sizes of miniatures given in inches are followed in brackets by the size in millimetres. Unless otherwise stated medium is watercolour on ivorine.

1. **MARGARET ADAMS HS ARMS**
   a. MALAYAN COURT DANCERS 6″ × 5″ (152 × 127 mm)
   b. MY GRANDMOTHER - MRS STURGEON 3¼″ × 4⅜″ (83 × 110 mm)
   c. HARRY - A VICTORIAN CHILD 4″ × 5″ (100 × 127 mm)

2. **PHYLLIS ARNOLD RMS PUSM PUSWA SM FIBA HS**
   (Transparencies kindly lent by owner)
   a. ASHLEY JONES Watercolour on vellum 3″ × 2½″ (76 × 64 mm)
   b. THOMAS CORRAN Watercolour on vellum 3″ × 2½″ (76 × 64 mm)
   c. THE CHOIRBOY Gouache on plaster 4″ × 3″ (100 × 76 mm)

3. **JENNY BROOKS DIP.AD ATC HS**
   a. QUINTON BROOKS Pencil on paper 6″ × 4¾″ (150 × 120 mm)
   b. RUTH GRENFELL-HILL Pencil on paper 3¾″ × 2¾″ (95 × 70 mm)

4. **WILHELMINA M. BURDETT-SOMERS ARMS MAA HS**
   a. A STREET SCENE IN PETRA, MAJORCA II Oil on copper 4½″ × 4½″ (114 × 114 mm)
   b. LINCOLN CATHEDRAL Oil on copper 4½″ × 4½″ (114 × 114 mm)

5. **JENNIFER BUXTON RMS HS**
   a. JOAN 9H pencil on ivory 3¼″ × 2¾″ (83 × 70 mm)
   b. LARA Watercolour on ivory 2½″ × 2″ (approx) (63 × 50 mm)
   c. ELIZABETH Watercolour on ivory 3″ × 2⅝″ (75 × 67 mm)

6. **HEATHER O. CATCHPOLE RMS HS**
   (Transparencies by Julian Comrie)
   a. KIRBY Watercolour on ivorine 2¼″ × 3″ (57 × 77 mm)
   b. GET OFF WHAT SOFA ? (Staged) Watercolour on ivorine 2¼″ × 2¾″ (57 × 72 mm)
   c. WINTER GALES Watercolour on ivorine 2½″ × 2″ (63 × 51 mm)

7. **SYLVIA CAVE MA HS**

a. RED ADMIRAL ON BRAMBLE Watercolour on vellum 4″ × 5″ (100 × 127 mm)

b. TOAD AND TOADSTOOL Watercolour on vellum 3″ × 4″ (76 × 100 mm)

c. CRANEFLY ON MICHAELMAS DAISIES Watercolour on vellum 2″ × 3″ (50 × 77 mm)

8. **LOVEDA COX HS**

a. MALLARDS Gouache on paper 1¼″ × 2⅞″ (32 × 74 mm)

b. VIEW OF WALLINGFORD ACROSS THE THAMES Watercolour and gouache on paper 3″ × 3″ (76 × 76 mm)

9. **PAMELA DAVIS VPRMS FSBA SWA HS**

a. LONDON DOORWAYS, BERKELEY SQUARE Transparency kindly lent by Llewellyn Alexander (Fine Paintings) Ltd. Acrylic and gouache on ivorine 4″ × 2¾″ (102 × 72 mm)

b. COUNTRY KITCHEN Transparency kindly lent by Llewellyn Alexander (Fine Paintings) Ltd. Acrylic and gouache on ivorine 4″ × 3¼″ (102 × 83 mm)

c. MIXED SPRING FLOWERS Acrylic on gouache on ivorine 4″ × 3″ (102 × 76 mm)

10. **PAULINE DENYER Des.RCA HS SLm**

a. DAME PEGGY ASHCROFT Watercolour on ivorine 2½″ × 3″ (on cover) (61 × 76 mm)

b. PORTRAIT OF SHELLEY (After Samuel) 2½″ × 3″ (61 × 76 mm)

11. **PHOEBE SHOLTO DOUGLAS RMS SWA HS**

a. MY MOTHER IN 1905 Watercolour on ivorine 4½″ × 6″ (114 × 152 mm)

b. LAWSON WOOD - MY FATHER Watercolour on ivorine 3″ × 4″ (76 × 102 mm)

c. RACHEL (Staged) each 2″ × 2½″ (51 × 63 mm)

12. **SHEILA FAIRMAN RMS FSBA SWA HS**

a. CHELSEA BUNS Oil on ivorine 4½″ × 3¼ (116 × 83 mm)

b. TEA FOR TWO Oil on ivorine 4¼″ × 3½″ (110 × 89 mm)

c. ICEBERG ROSE AND STRAWBERRIES Oil on ivorine (on cover) 3″ × 4″ (76 × 102 mm)

13. **ELAINE FELLOWS ARMS SWA HS**

a. MR CARTER OF HARBORNE (Artist's Private Collection) 3″ × 2½″ (76 × 61 mm)
b. WHISPERS Kindly loaned by Mr & Mrs G. F. Thomas 2½″ × 2″ (61 × 50 mm)
c. CRABE BISQUE Transparency kindly loaned by Llewellyn Alexander Gallery, London Watercolour on vellum 5⅞″ × 3½″ (150 × 90 mm)

14. **ROBERT HUGHES RMS HS**

a. HYDRANGEAS Oil on board (on cover) 3⅞″ × 2⅞″ (100 × 72 mm)
b. WINTER SUNSHINE Oil on board 3⅞″ × 2⅞″ (100 × 72 mm)
c. A CORNER OF KENNET Oil on board 3⅞″ × 2⅞″ (100 × 72 mm)

15. **Cmdr. G. W. G. HUNT RN ARMS HS**

a. 'SINGEING THE KING'S BEARD' Sir Francis Drake attacked the Spanish Fleet at Cadiz with Fire Ships. Acrylic on antique snuff box. 3″ × 2″ (76 × 51 mm)
b. BARGES AT OLD CHELSEA Acrylic on antique snuff box 1½″ × 2½″ (38 × 64 mm)
c. HMS WARRIOR OFF GIBRALTAR Acrylic on antique snuff box 1¼″ × 2¼″ (32 × 58 mm)

16. **JOAN JOYCE SLm HS**

a. THE DUKE OF WELLINGTON (From original by Richard Crossway) Watercolour 3½″ × 2½″ (89 × 64 mm)
b. TABBY KITTEN (loaned by owner) Gouache and watercolour 4″ diameter (100 mm dia.)

17. **MEG KINGSTON HS**

a. COMMON BLUE AT LANGTON MATRAVERS (on back cover) 3″ × 2⅛″ (76 × 54 mm)
b. PIGGY 3½″ × 2⅜″ (89 × 60 mm)
c. OWL 2″ × 2½″ (50 × 64 mm)

18. **ELISABETH LAKE RMS HS**

Both are watercolour on Ivorex

a. SUNLIT PASSAGE 2″ × 3²⁄₁₁″ (51 × 82 mm)
b. BLUEBELLS 2″ × 3²⁄₁₀ (51 × 82 mm)

19. **DAPHNE LEE RMS HS**

Transparencies kindly lent by Artist

a. PIGS 3″ × 2½″ (76 × 63 mm)
b. TEDDIES 2½″ × 3″ (63 × 76 mm)
c. SQUIRRELS 2½″ × 3″ (63 × 76 mm)

20. **SUZANNE LUCAS FLS PRMS FPSBA SWA Hon.HS**

Watercolour on ivory that is 40 years old

a. SEEDS AND LEAVES AND TINY TOADSTOOLS (on cover) 3″ × 4″ (76 × 102 mm)

b. ALPINE FLOWERS 3″ × 4″ (76 × 102 mm)

c. CONIFERS AND MAPLE SEEDS 3½″ × 5″ (89 × 127 mm)

21. **ERIC MORTON ARMS HS**

a. FOLLOW ME GIRLS Watercolour (Kindly loaned by Mrs P. Colver) 2⁹⁄₁₆″ × 1¹¹⁄₁₆″ (66 × 44 mm)

b. THE SHOW TEAM (Kindly lent by Jillian Llewellyn-Lloyd) 2″ × 3″ (51 × 76 mm)

22. **W. P. MUNDY RMS FCSD HS**

All are watercolour on ivory

a. JOCKEY JAMES CARTER (Staged)

b. THE GONG OF MALAYSIA 3½″ × 3″ (89 × 76 mm)

c. JULIA FOWLER (on back cover) 3¾″ × 3″ (95 × 76 mm)

23. **MAUREEN PEARSON HS**

Watercolour and gouache on white card

a. WOBURN WALK IN THE RAIN (HS – Best in Exhibition 1990) 4″ × 3″ (100 × 76 mm)

b. COURTYARD, PALAZZO VECCHIO 2½″ × 3¼″ (64 × 82 mm)

c. BLACK IRIS (SWAHILI) 2½″ × 3″ (64 × 76 mm)

24. **MICHAEL PIERCE Profilist and Silhouettist**

a. YOUNG GIRL 3″ × 2″ (76 × 51 mm)

b. GROUP CAPTAIN W. D. DAVID CBE DFC AFC 3″ × 2″ (76 × 51 mm)

c. SPITFIRE 3½″ × 1¼″ (89 × 32 mm)

25. **ROSALIND PIERSON RMS HS (Founder) MMAS**

Watercolour on Bristol board

a. RIVER TAVY, DEVON 4″ × 3⅗ (102 × 90 mm)

b. DARTMOOR SCENE 3½″ × 2⅞″ (89 × 72 mm)

c. EVENING LIGHT 3⅗ × 2½″ (90 × 64 mm)

26. **JOYCE ROGERSON RMS SWA MASF USM**

a. CHAFFINCH Watercolour on ivorine 2½″ × 3″ (64 × 76 mm)

b. WRENS Watercolour on ivorine 2½″ × 3″ (64 × 76 mm)

27. **MARGARET RYDER VPRMS SWA FSBA HS SM**

a. Dr ERIC WALTER SKIPPER MD FRCP, London 3½″ × 4″ (89 × 100 mm)

b. WINTER FLOWERS (on cover) 3½″ × 3″ (89 × 76 mm)

c. FLOWERPIECE WITH YELLOW LILY 3¼″ × 3″ (83 × 76 mm)

28. **SHEILA SANFORD RI RMS**

Watercolour on vellum

a. KITTEN IN THE WINDOW 2½″ × 2″ (63 × 50 mm)
b. SUMMER FIELDS 2½″ × 2″ (63 × 50 mm)
c. FIVE DUCKS 2½″ × 2″ (63 × 50 mm)

29. **HENRY SAXON RMS HS**

Watercolour and gouache/gold leaf on vellum and ivorine

a. PSALM 121 4½″ × 3″ (114 × 76 mm)
b. I VOW TO THEE MY COUNTRY 4½″ × 3½″ (114 × 89 mm)
c. TREASURE (on cover) 3⅛″ × 2½″ (80 × 64 mm)

30. **SYDNEY SHORTHOUSE RMS HS**

All watercolour on ivory

a. MRS FLORRIE SHORTHOUSE In the collection of her daughter, Mrs B. Willars. 2½″ × 3″ (63 × 76 mm)
b. MARCUS BRITTAIN In the collection of Mr & Mrs G. V. Brittain. 2½″ × 3″ (63 × 76 mm)
c. ALICE HOWARD In the collection of Capt. RN & Mrs C. V. Howard of Mollington, Oxon. 2½″ × 3″ (63 × 76 mm)

31. **BARBARA VALENTINE NDD ARMS HS SLm**

Transparencies kindly loaned by the artist.

a. WHO LOVES YOU, BABY? 4″ dia. (100 mm dia.)
b. MIDSUMMER'S EVE 4″ dia. (100 mm dia.)
c. ADA VALENTINE AND HER FAMILY 4″ × 5″ (100 × 127 mm)

32. **FLORENCE YOUNG SWA RMS**

Transparencies kindly loaned by the artist.

a. MODEL BOAT BEING BUILT AT BOAT BUILDING SHED, CHICHESTER, DELL QUAY Watercolour on vellum 4″ × 3″ (100 × 76 mm)
b. IN THE FOOTSTEPS OF SCOTT – ANTARCTIC EXPEDITION 1984-86 (Later the SOUTHERN QUEST) Watercolour on vellum 4¼″ × 3¼″ (109 × 82 mm)
c. THAMES BARGE AND CANAL BRIDGE AT ST KATHERINE'S DOCK BOAT MUSEUM Watercolour on vellum 4″ × 3″ (100 × 76 mm)

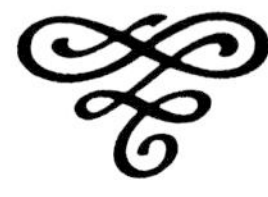

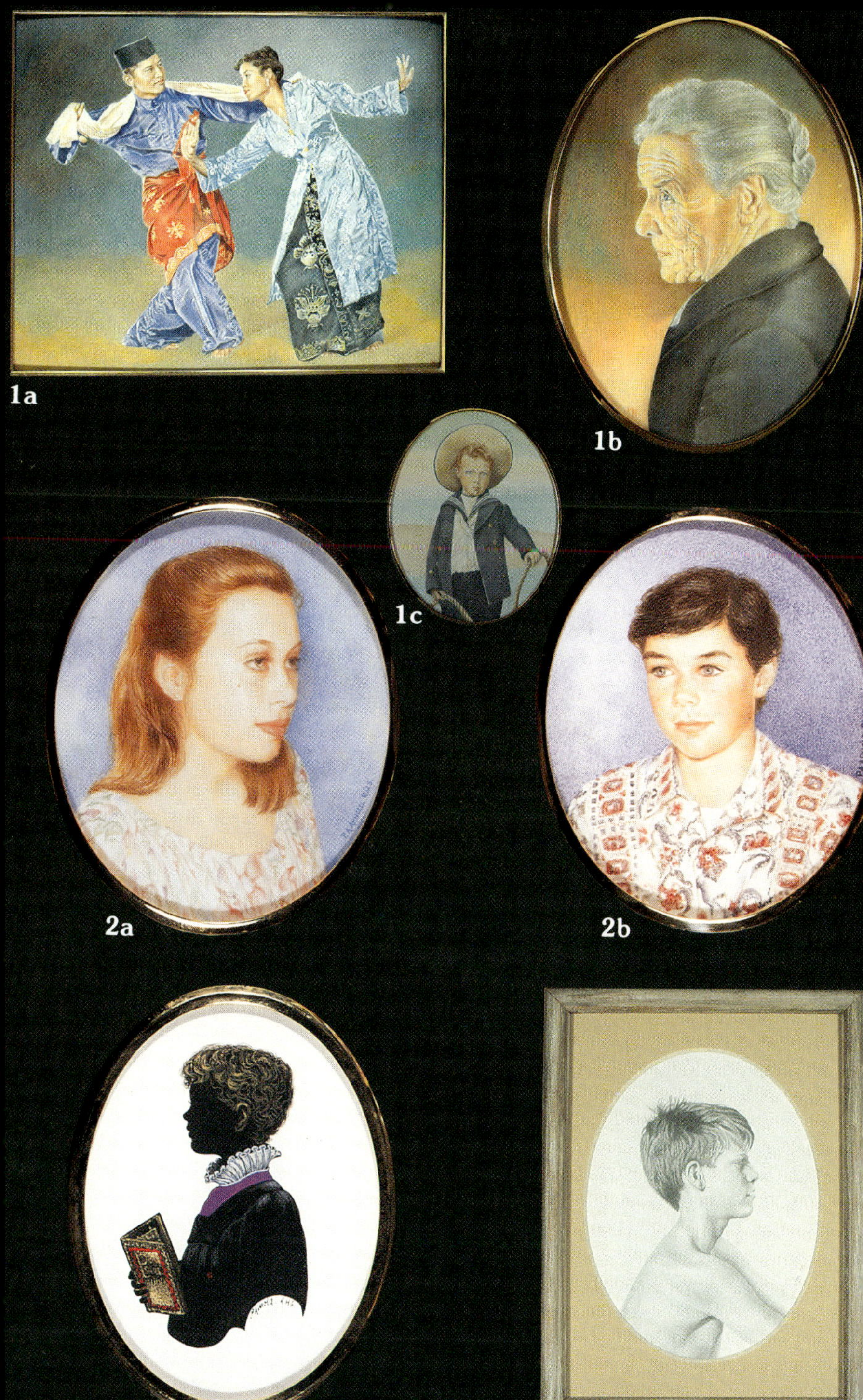
1a
1b
1c
2a
2b
2c
3a

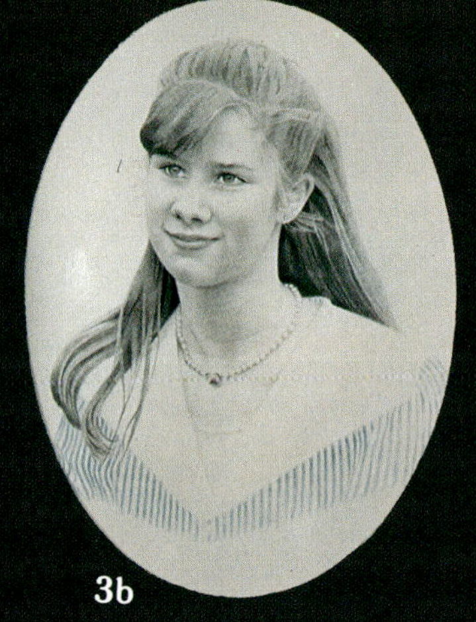
3b

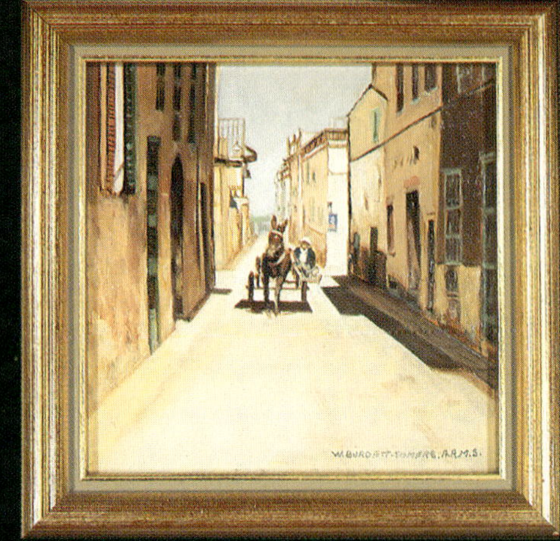

4a

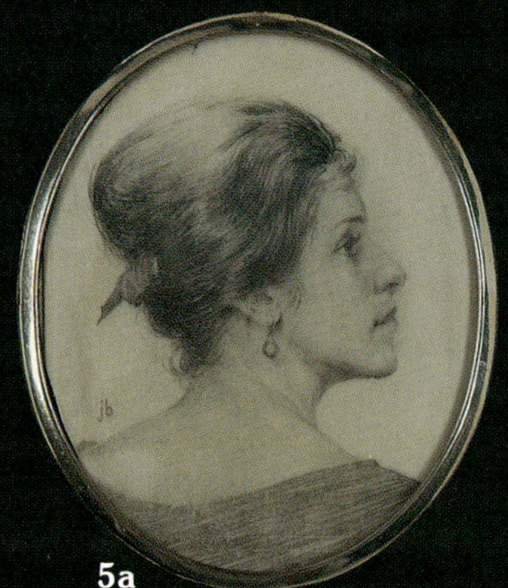

5a

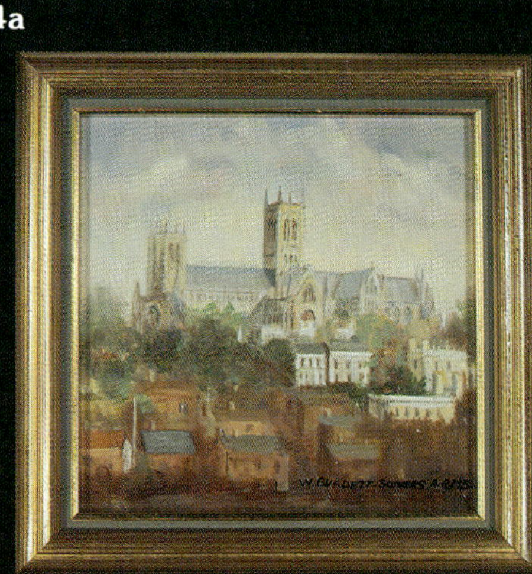

4b

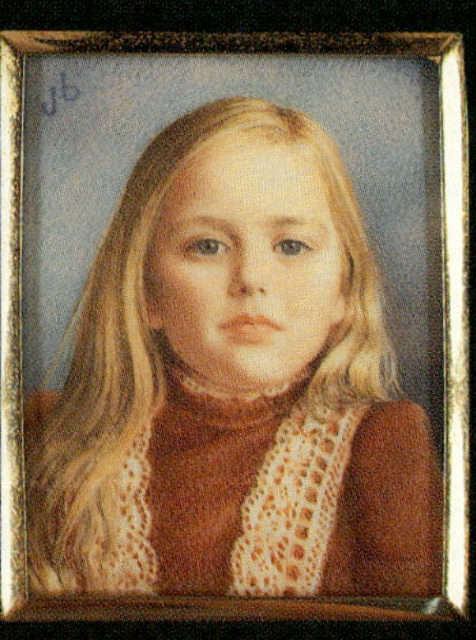
5b

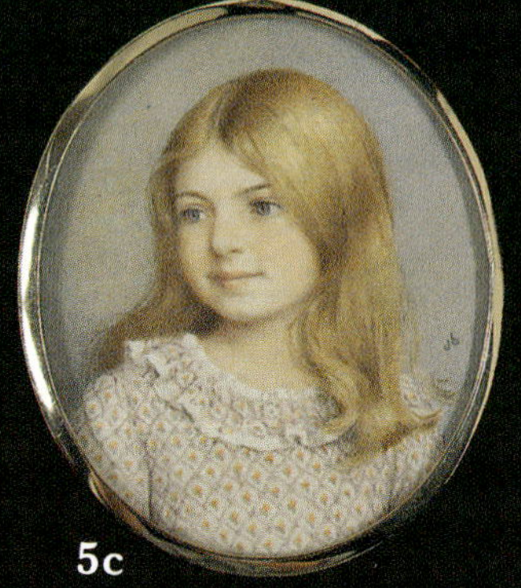
5c

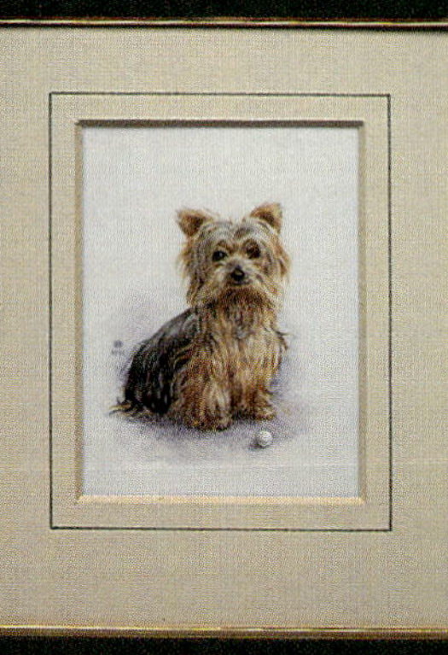
6a

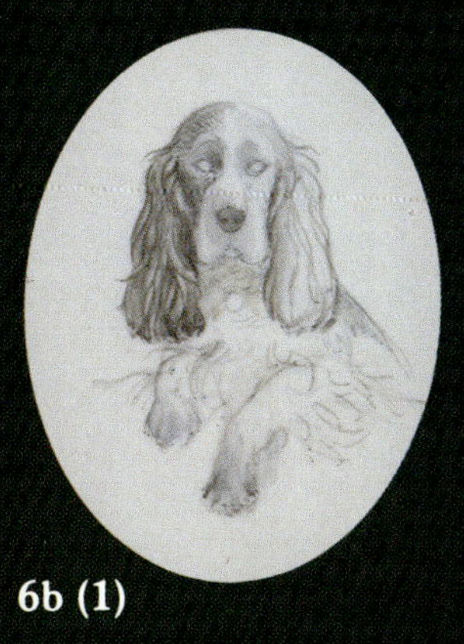
6b (1)

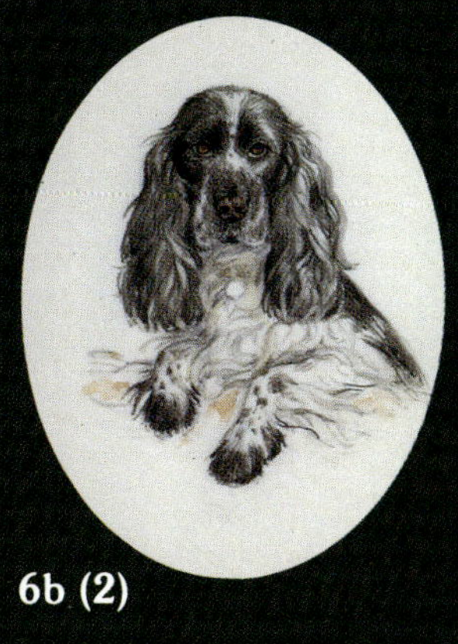
6b (2)

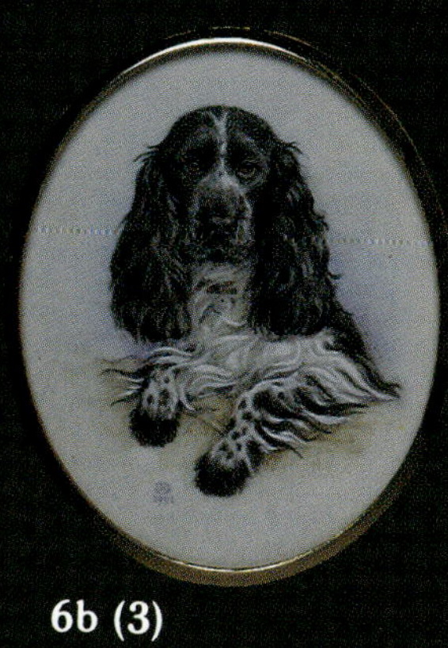
6b (3)

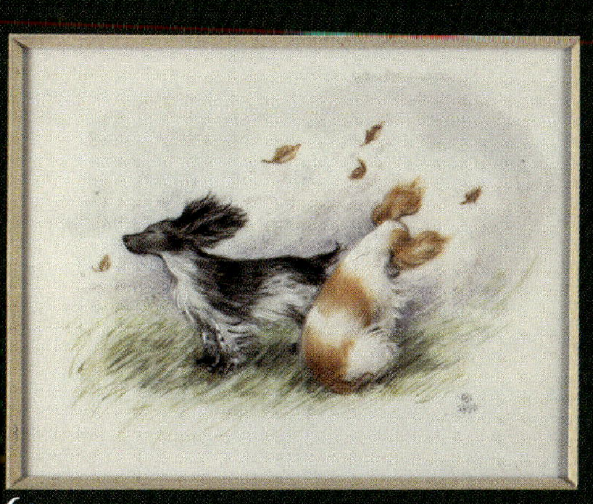
6c

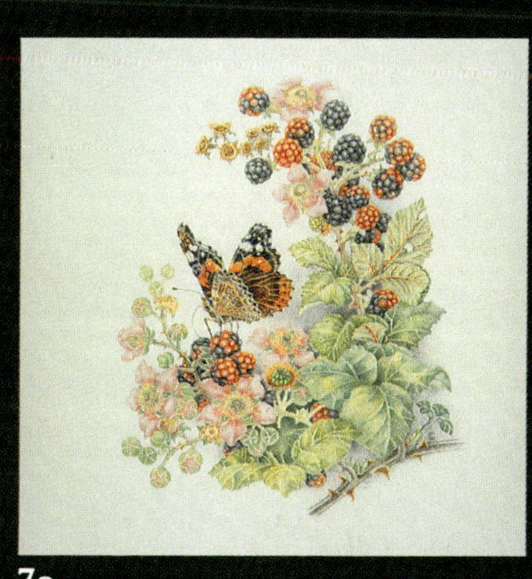
7a

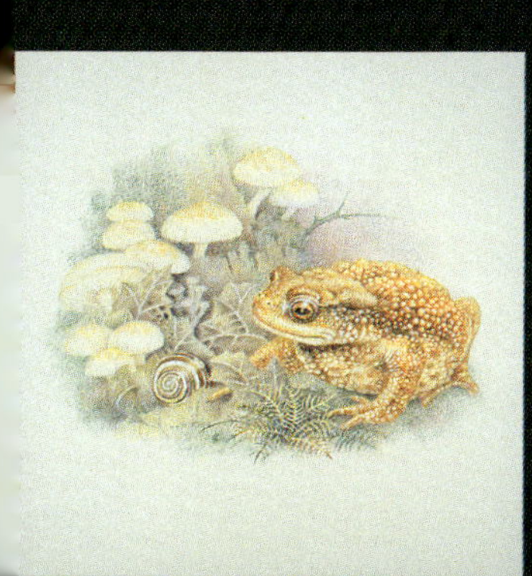
7b

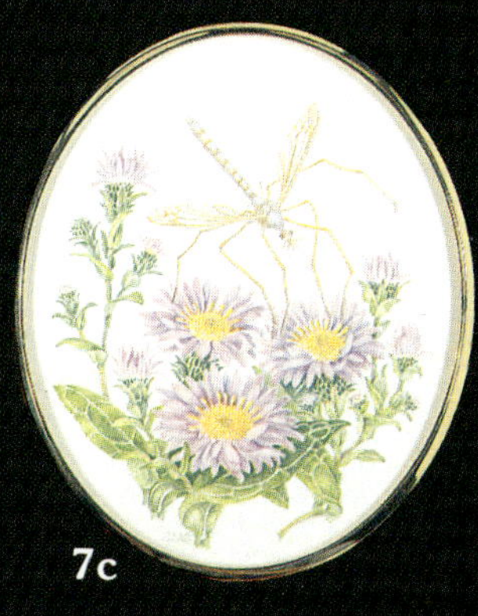
7c

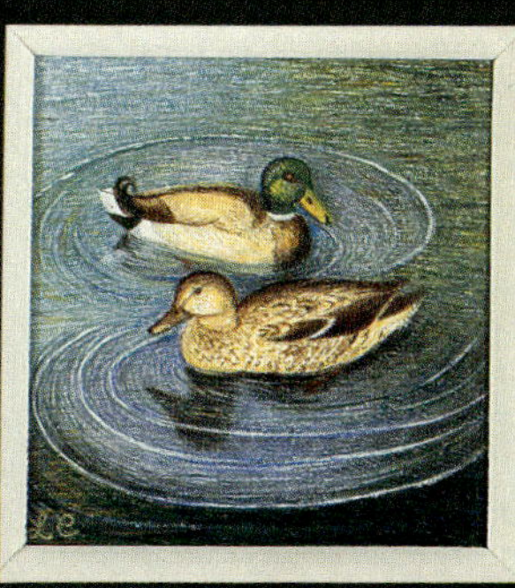
8a

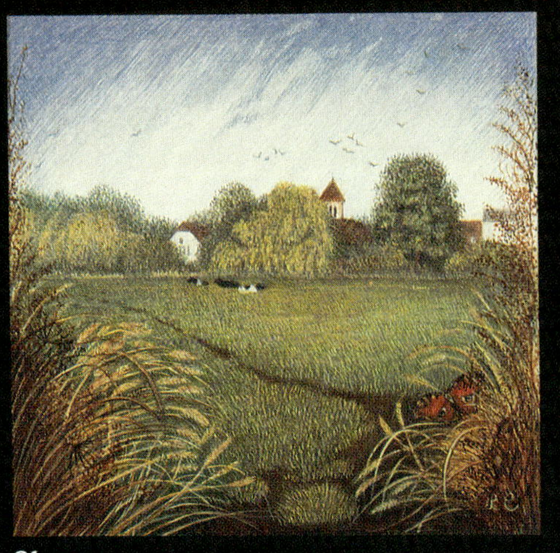

8b

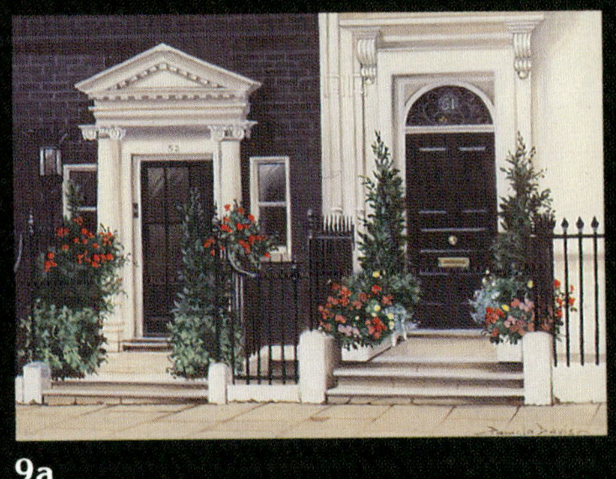

9a

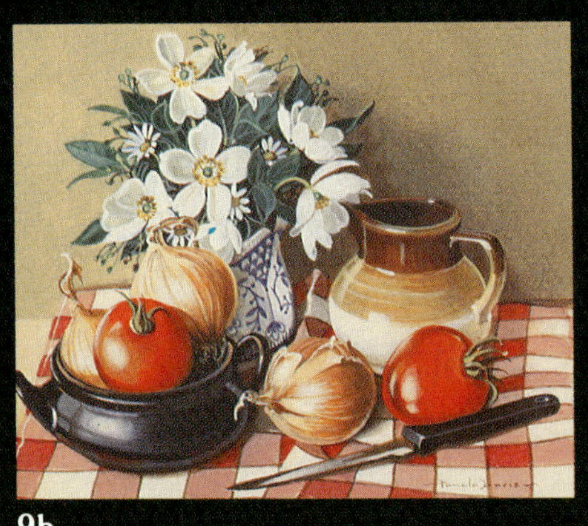

9b

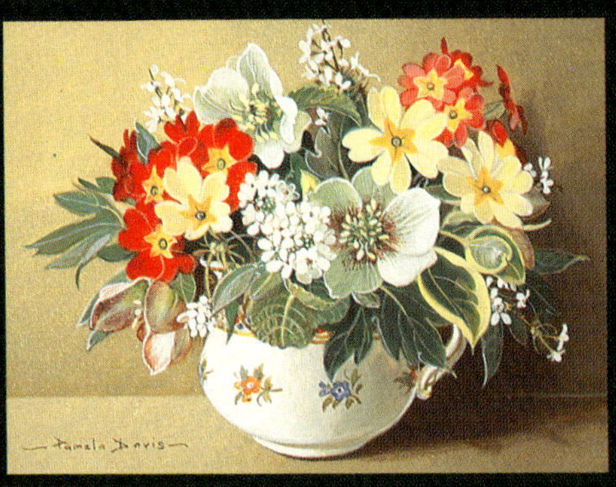

9c

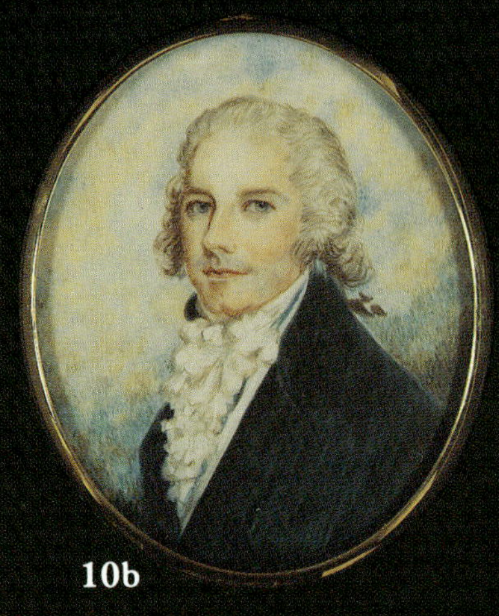

10b

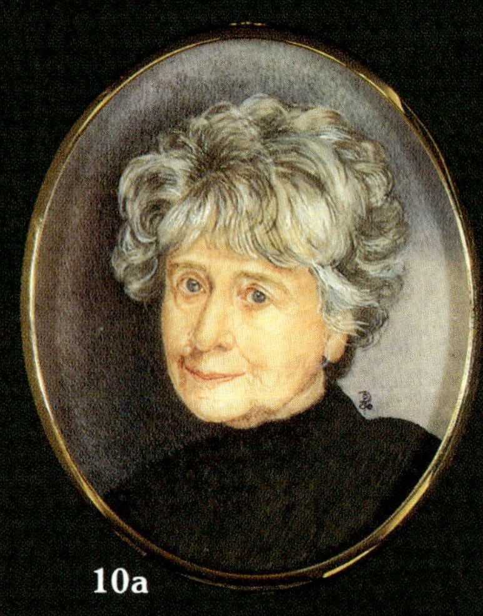

10a

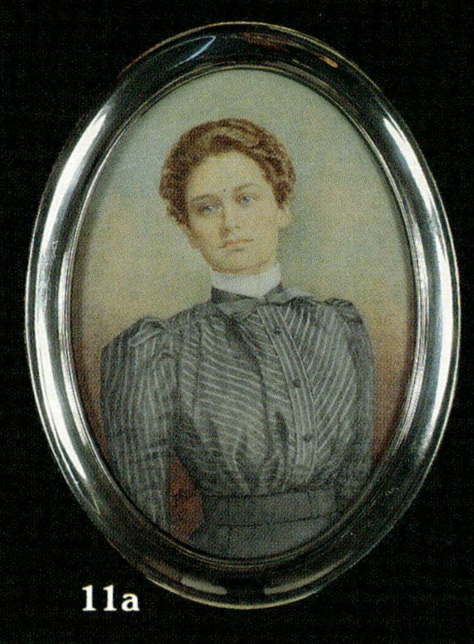

11a

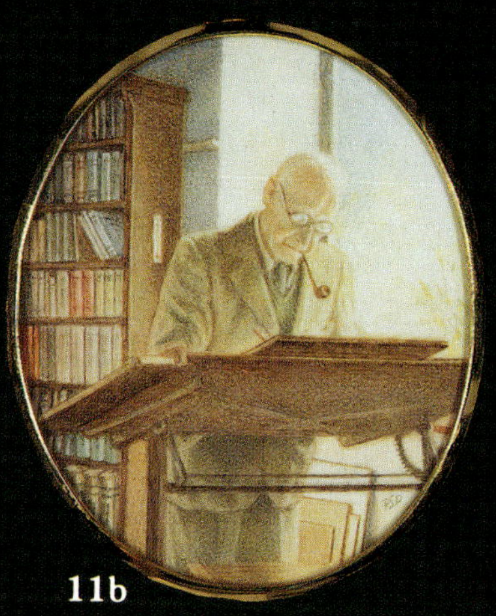

11b

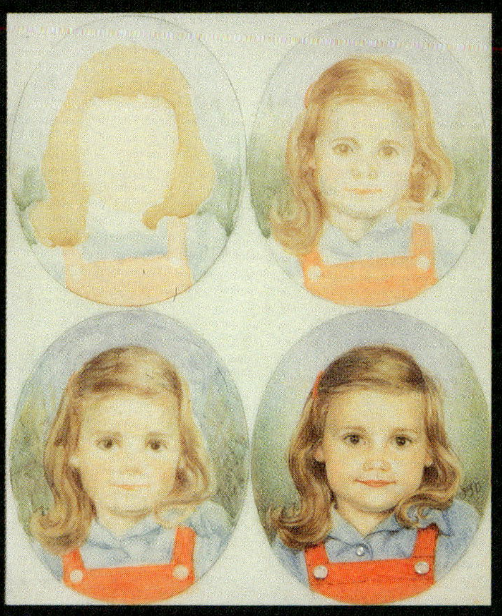

11c

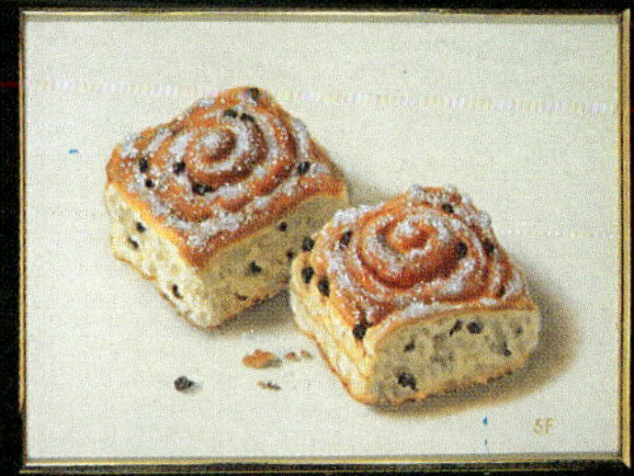

12a

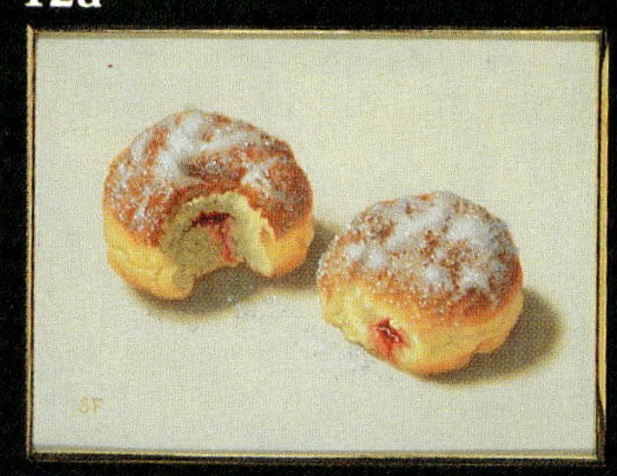

12b

12c

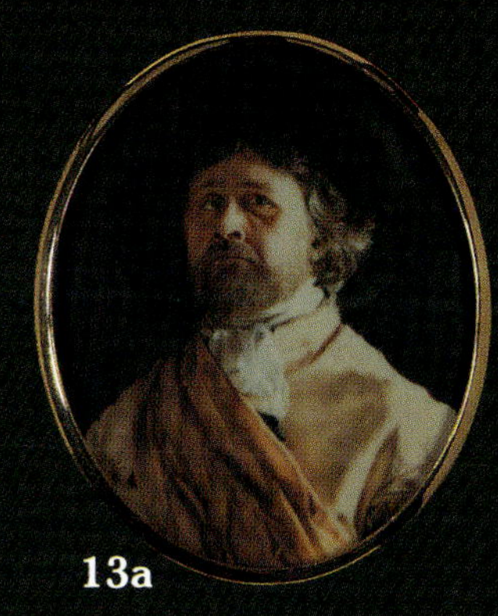

13a

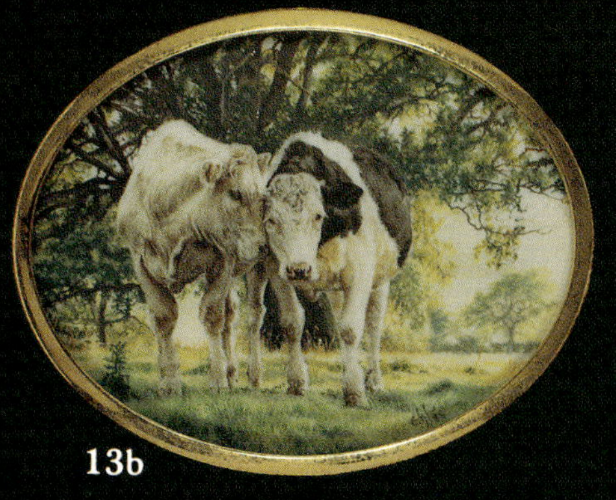
13b

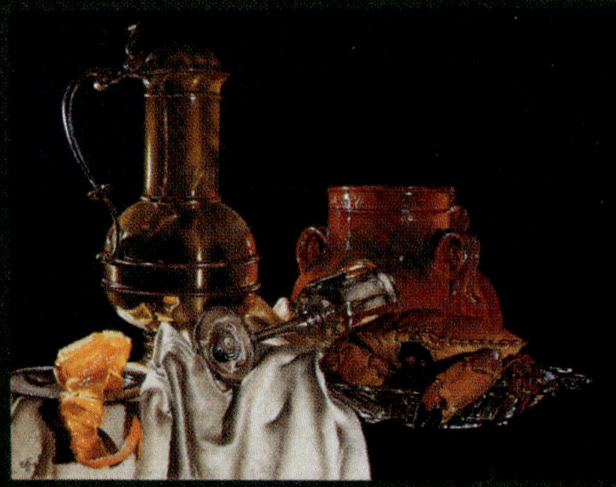
13c

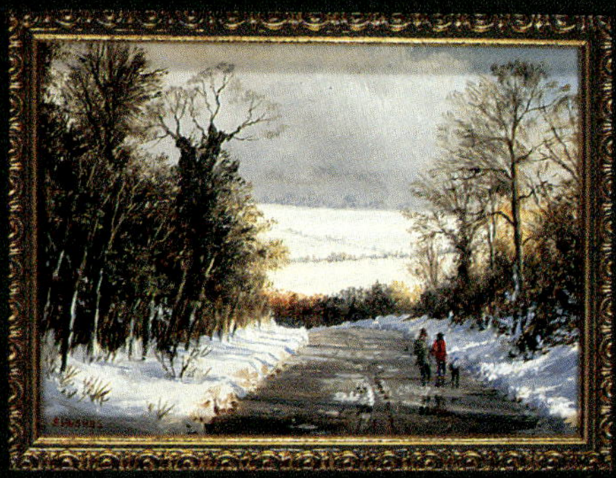
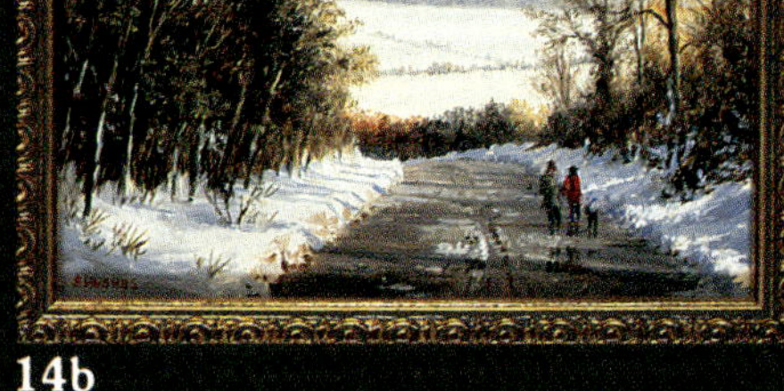
14b

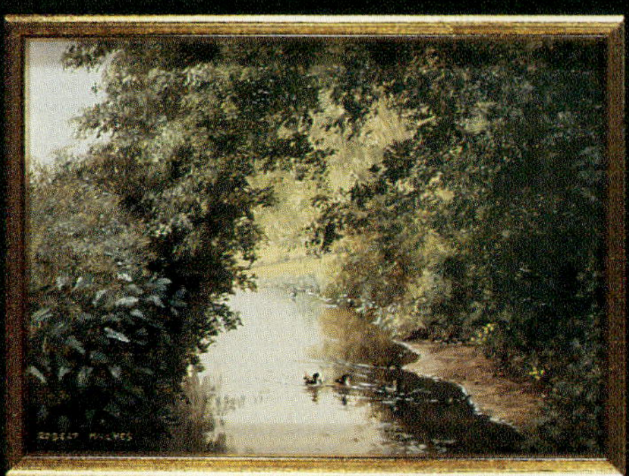
14c

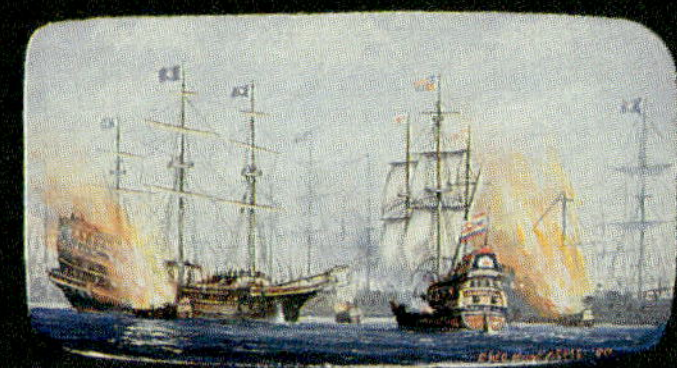
15a

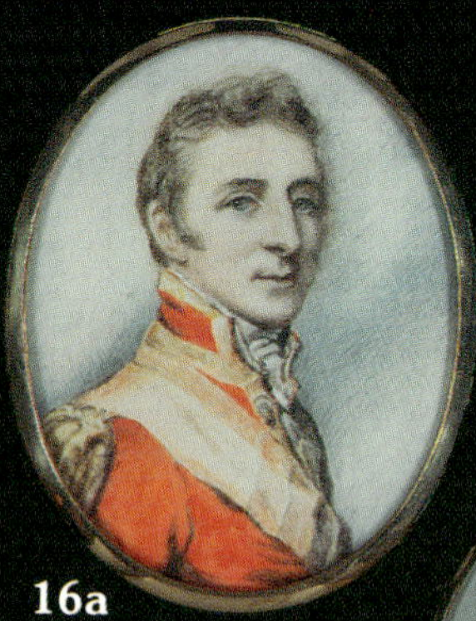

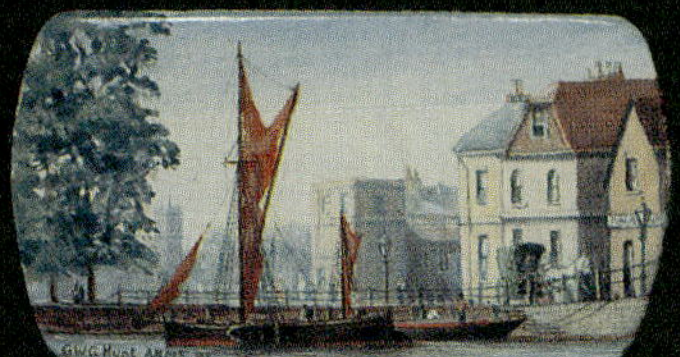
15b

16a

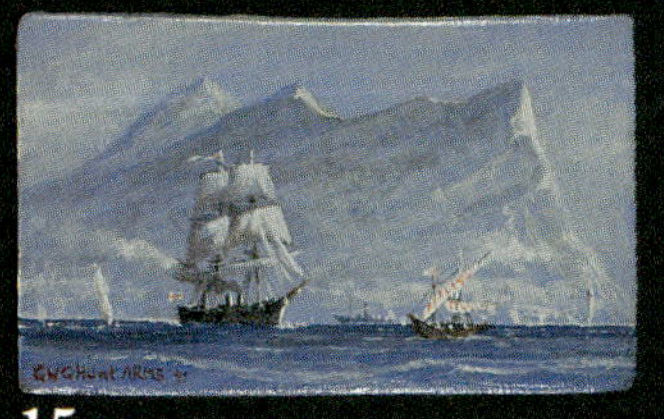
15c

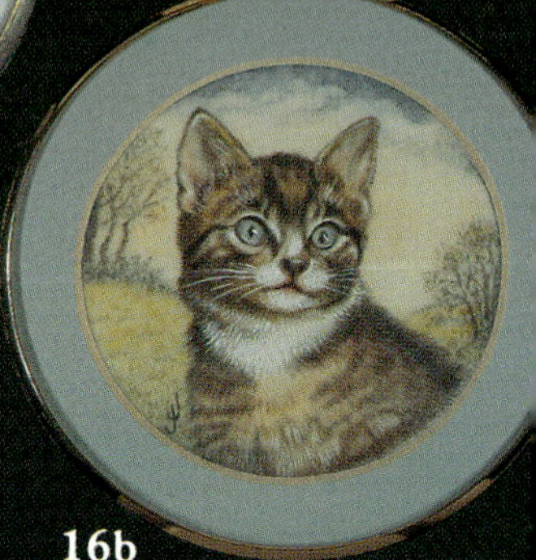
16b

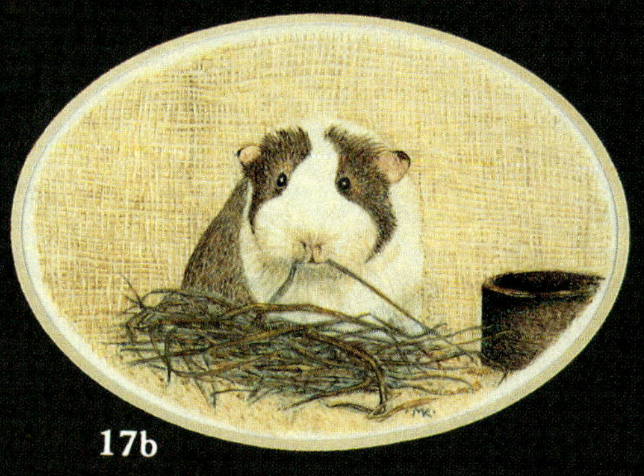

17b

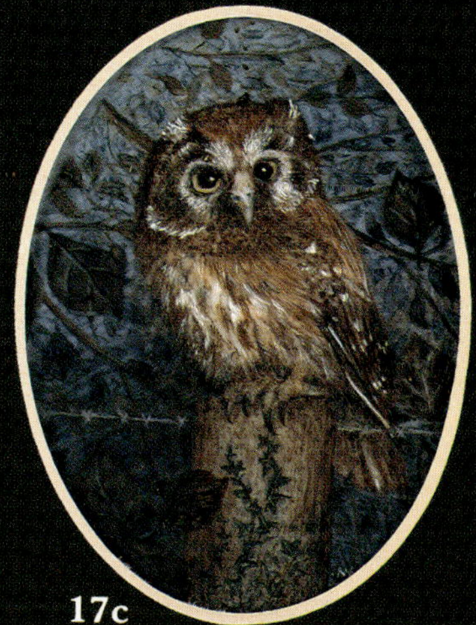

17c

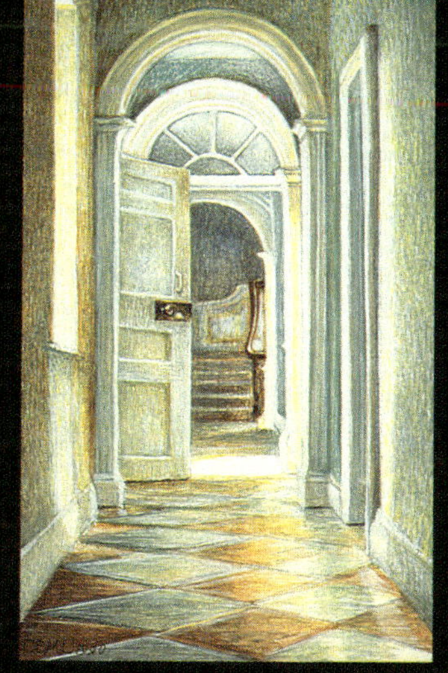

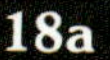

18a

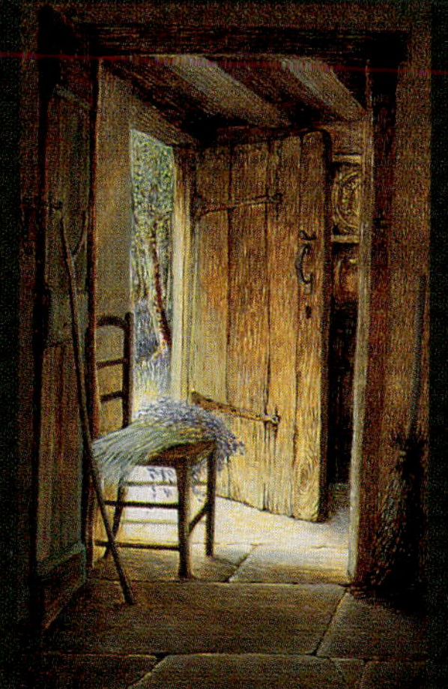

18b

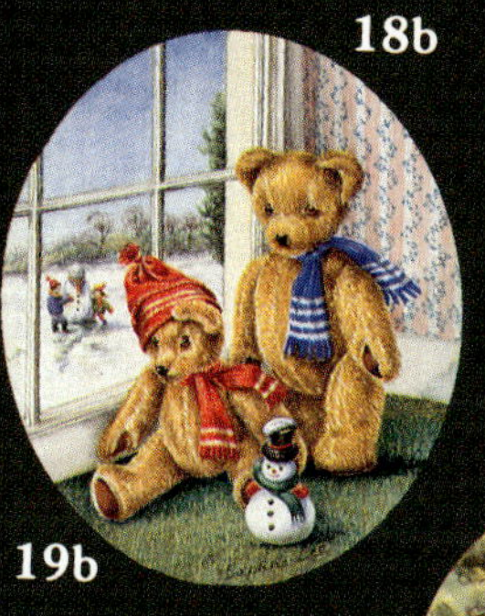

19b

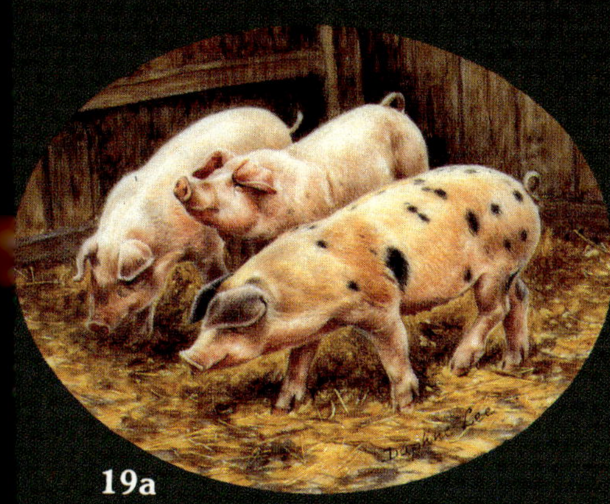

19a

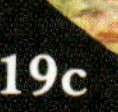

19c

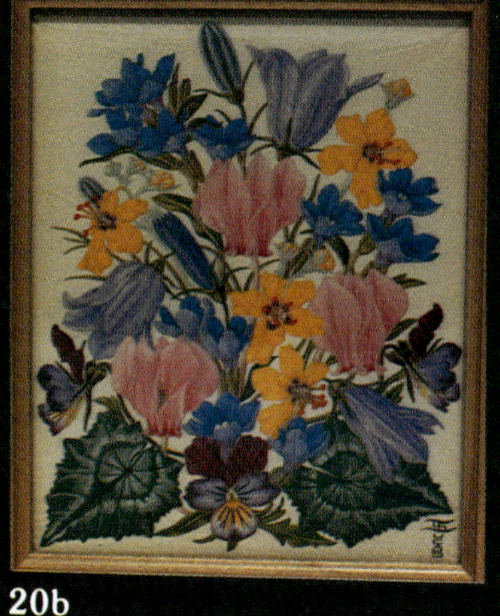
20b

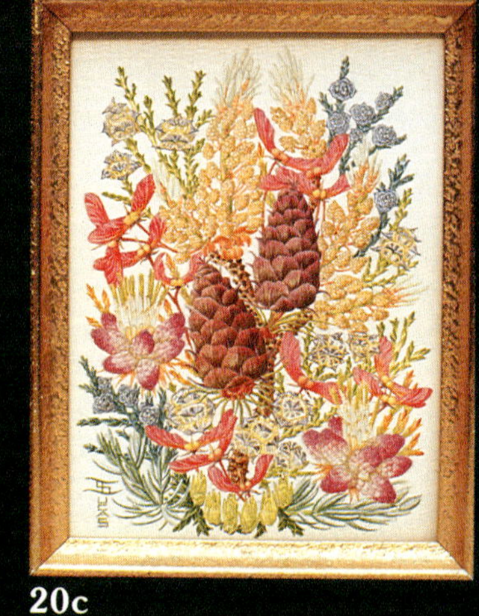
20c

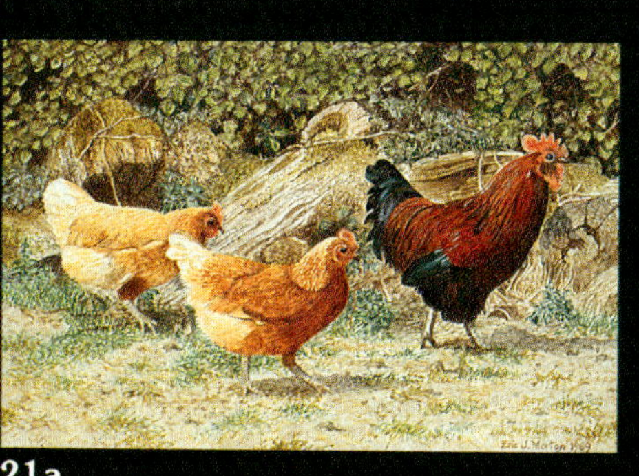
21a

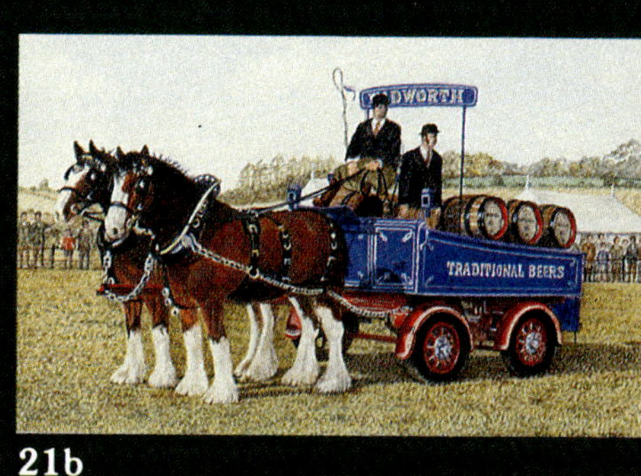

21b

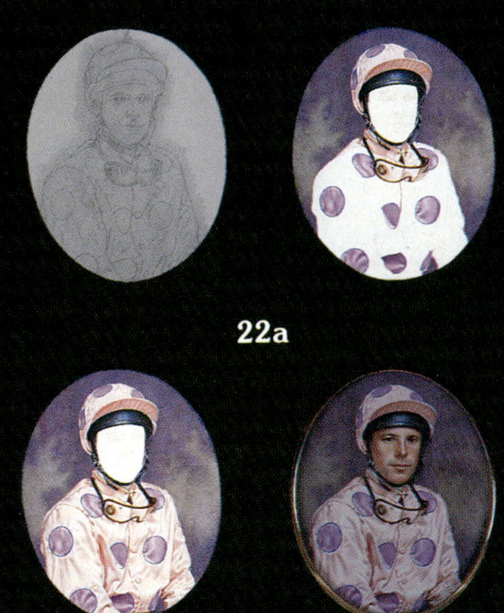
22a

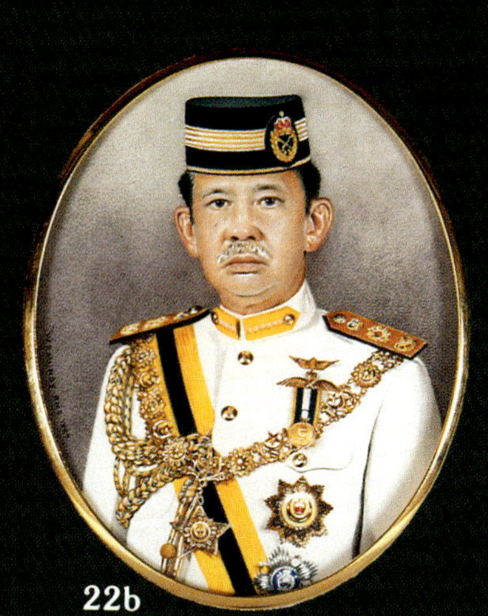
22b

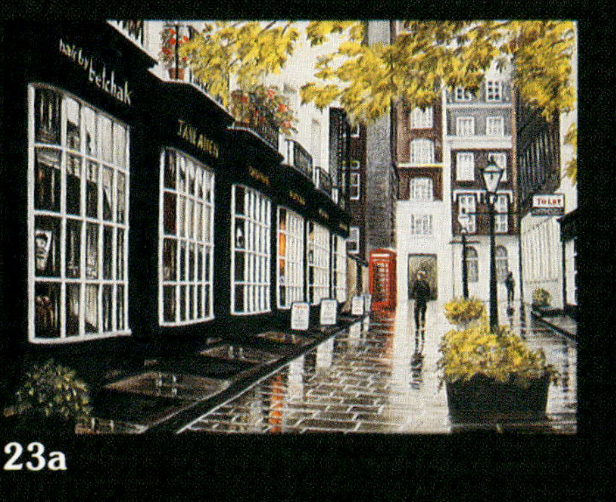

23a

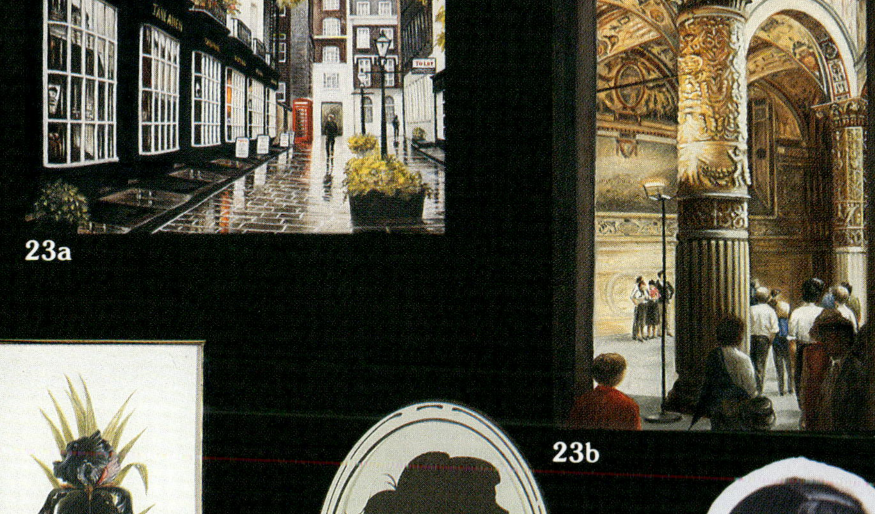

23b

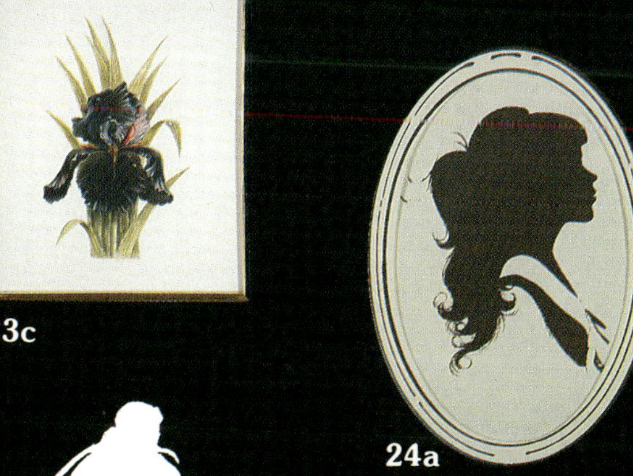

23c

24a

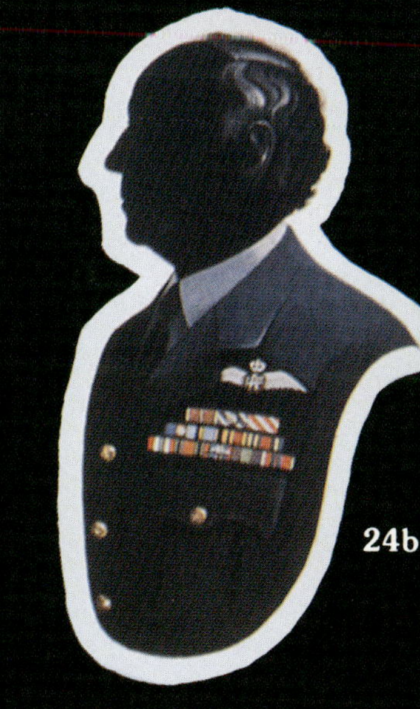

24b

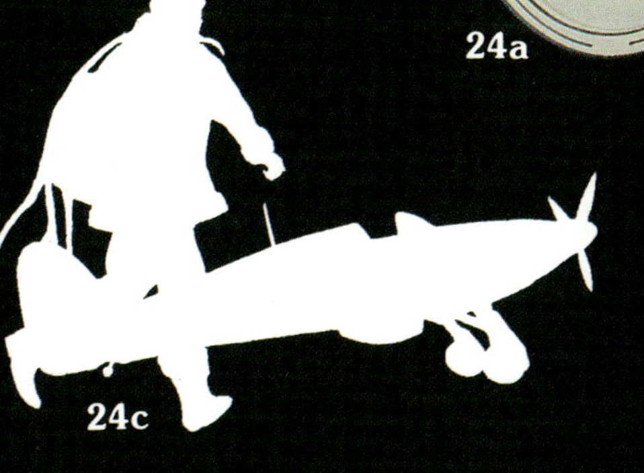

24c

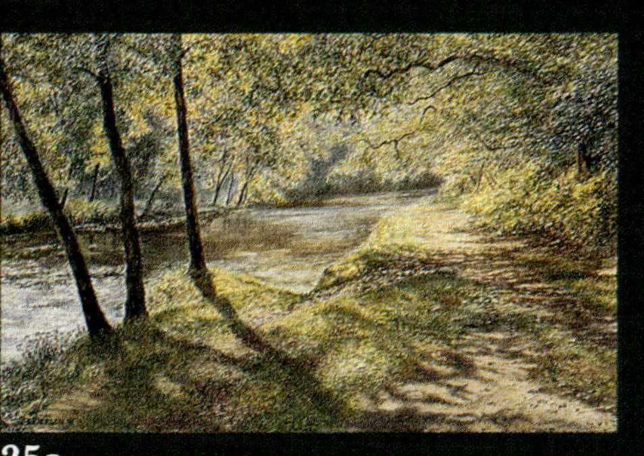

25a

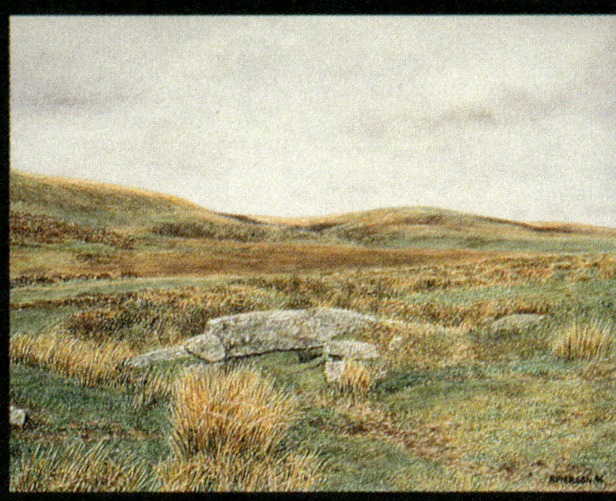

25b

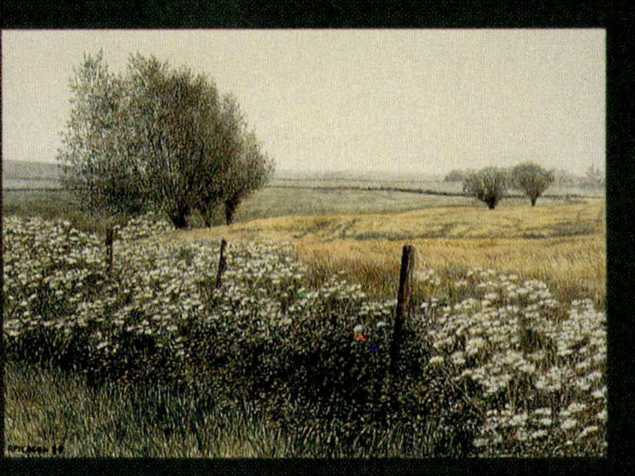

25c

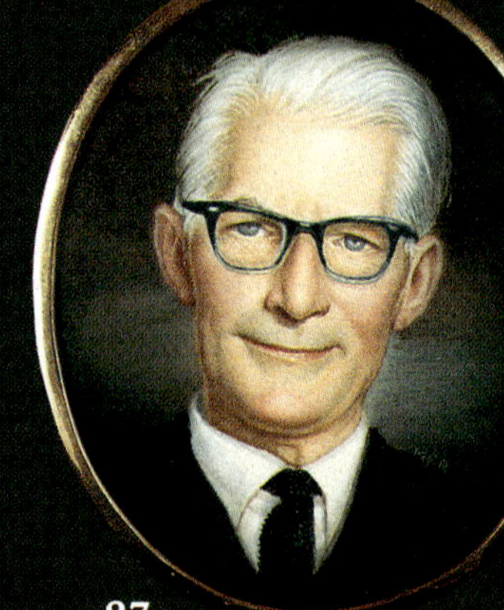

27a

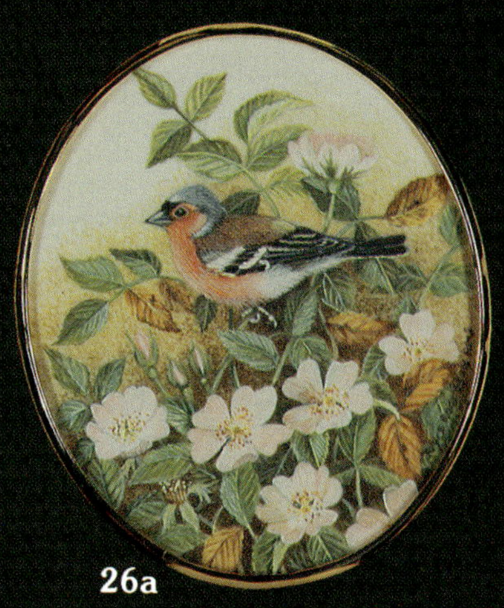

26a

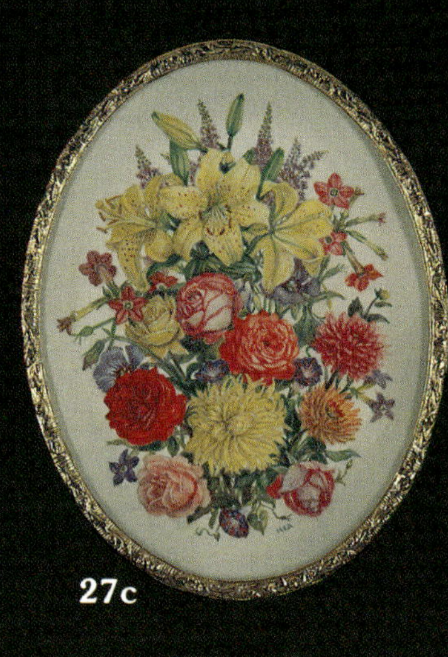

27c

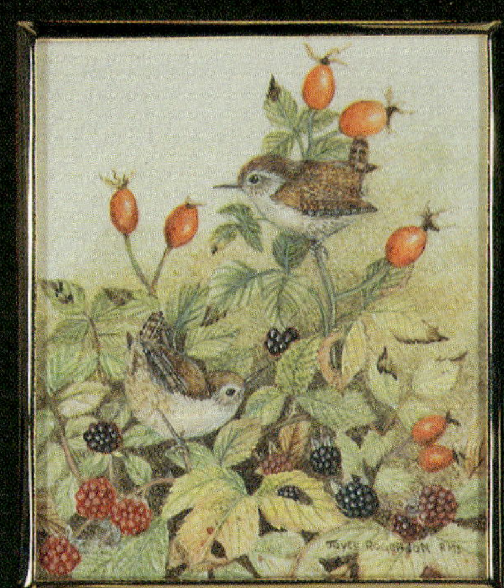

26b

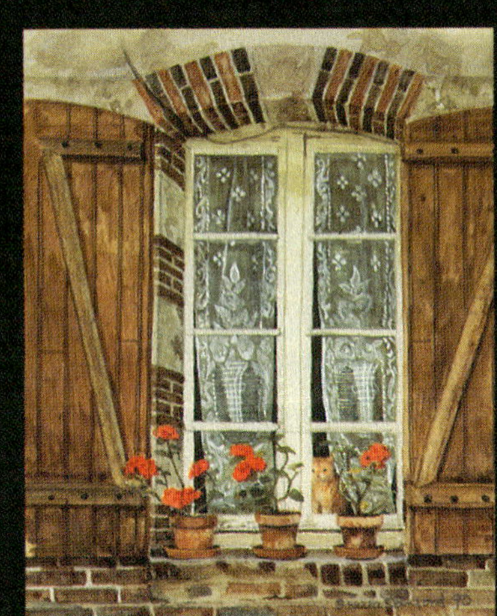

28a

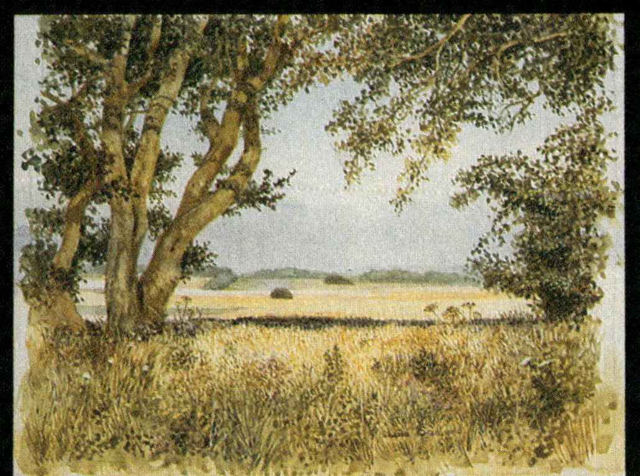

28b

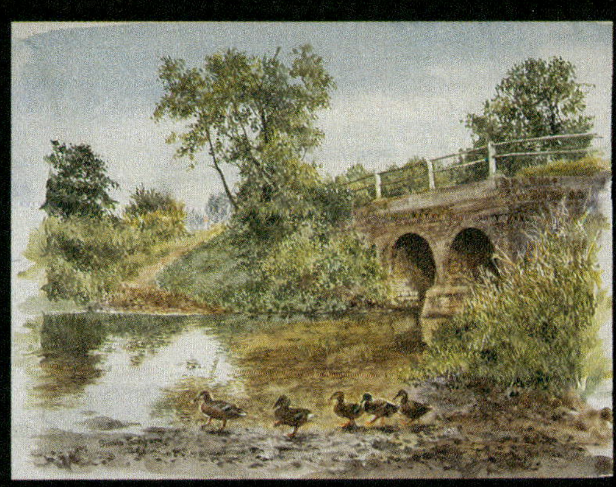

28c

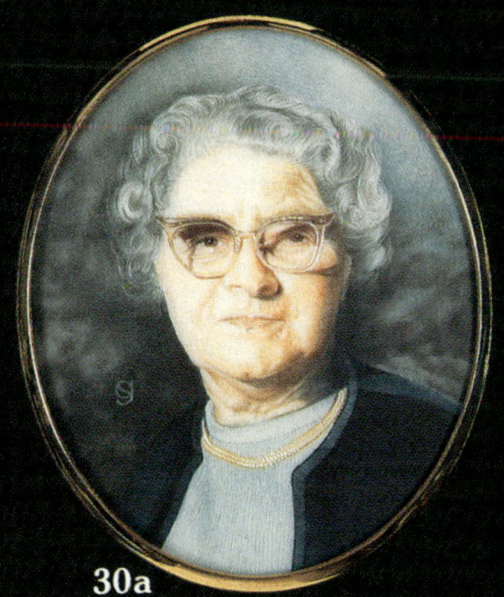

30a

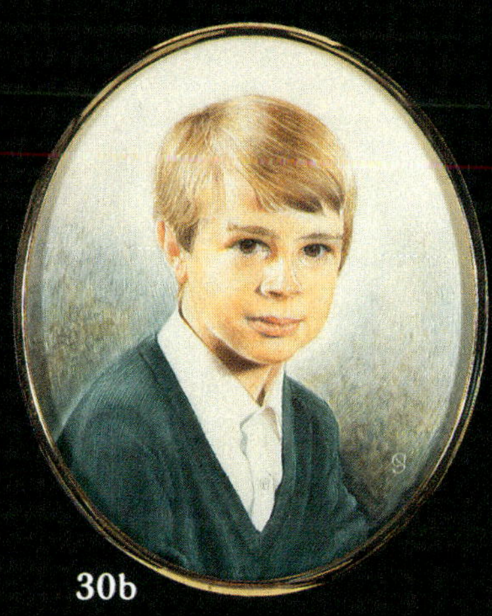

30b

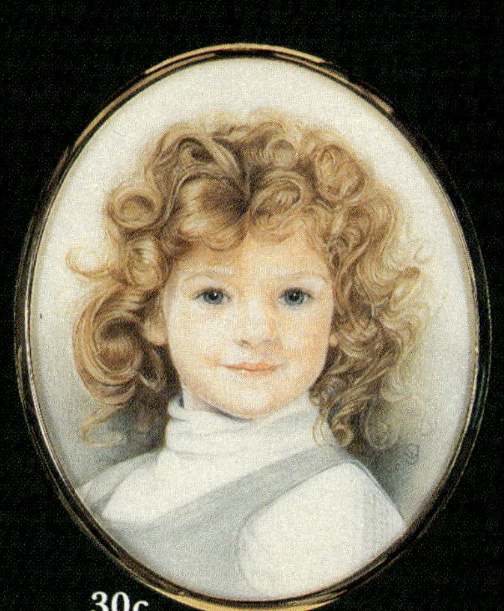

30c

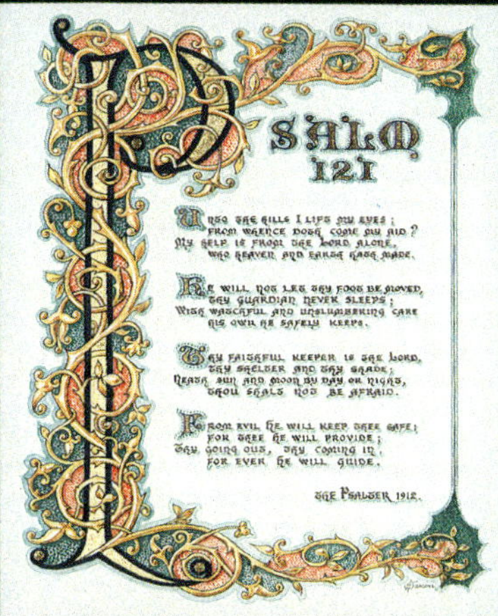

29a

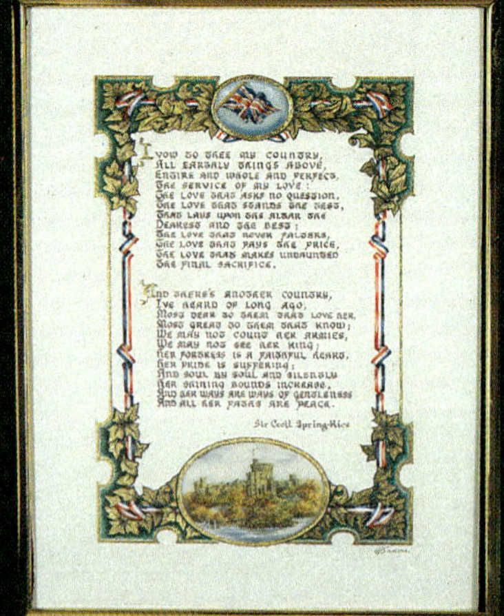

29b

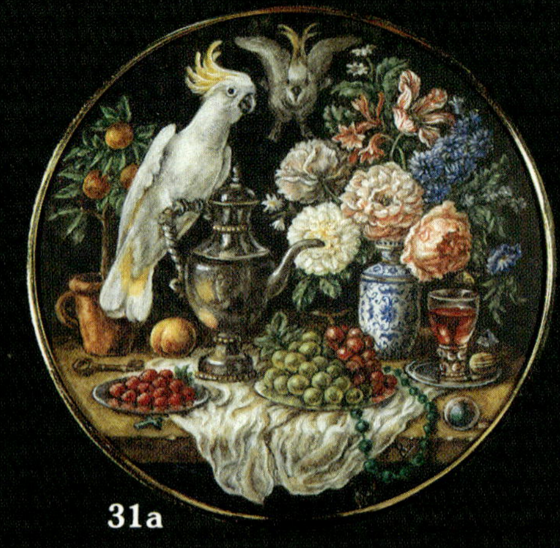

31a

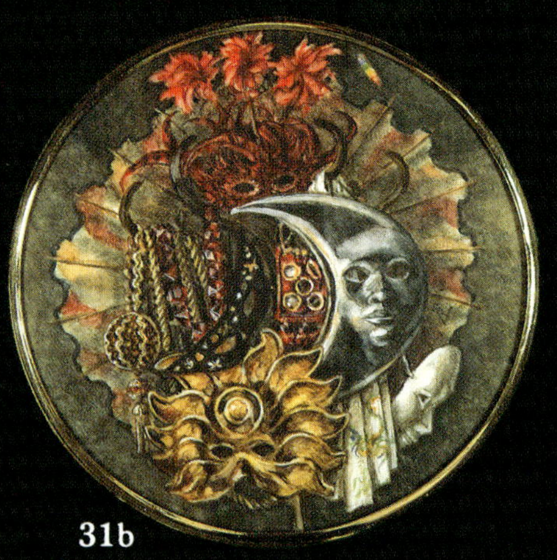

31b

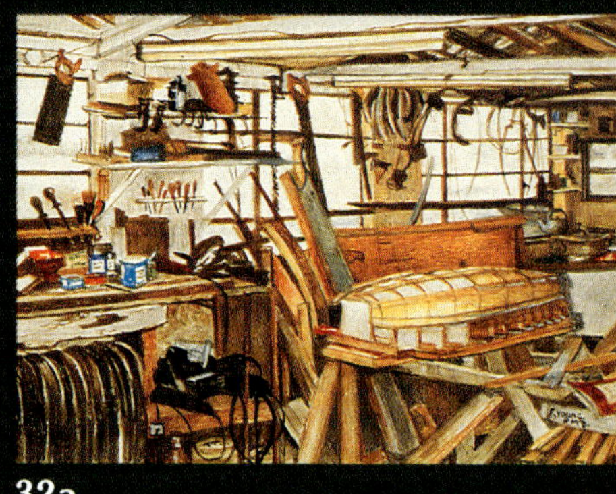

32a

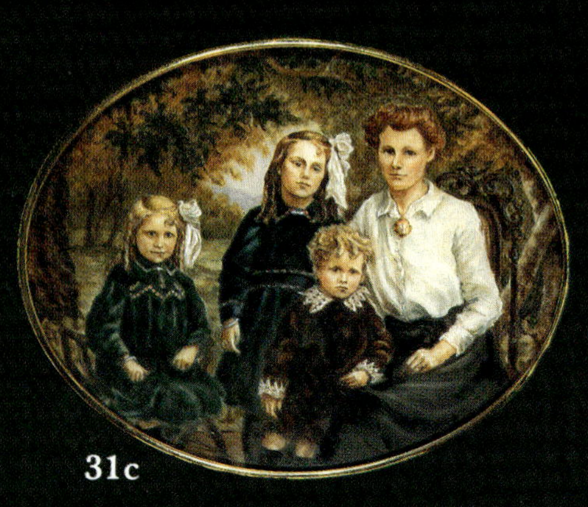

31c

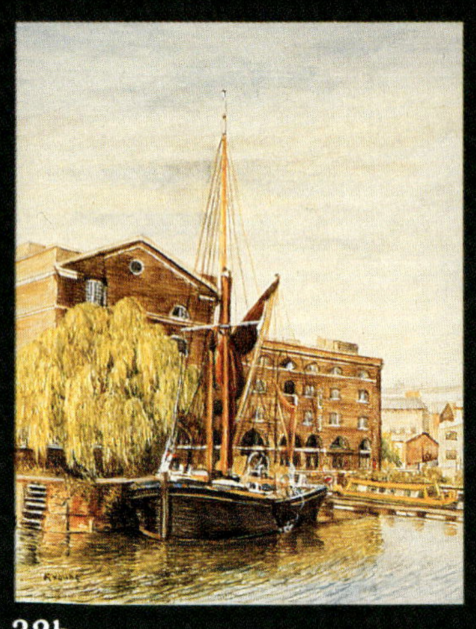

32b

Suggested Further Reading

John Smart: The Man and His Miniatures by Daphne Foskett (Cory, Adams & Mackay) 1964

British Portrait Miniatures by Daphne Foskett (Spring Books) 1983

British Silhouette Painters and Their Work 1760-1860 by Sue Mckechnie (Sotheby Parke Bernet) 1978

The English Miniature by John Murdoch, Jim Murrell, Patrick J. Noon and Roy Strong (Yale University Press) 1981

Hilliard & Oliver by Marie Edmond (Robert Hale) 1983

Painting for Calligraphers by Marie Angel (Pelham Books) 1984

The English Renaissance Miniature by Roy Strong (Thames & Hudson) 1983 and 1984

Catalogue of Portrait Miniatures in the Fitzwilliam Museum, Cambridge by Robert Bayne-Powell, C.B. (Cambridge University Press/Fitzwilliam Museum) 1985

Miniatures: A Dictionary and Guide by Daphne Foskett (Antique Collectors Club) 1987

These are but a few.

Helpful for beginners: *Painting Miniatures* by Elizabeth Davys Wood (A & C Black) 1989

Societies

The Hilliard Society, 15 Union Street, Wells, Somerset BA5 2PU

N.A.P.A. (National Acrylic Painters Association) 134 Rake Lane, Wallasey, Wirral L45 1JW, has an acrylic miniatures' section.

The Royal Society of Miniature Painters, Sculptors and Gravers, 17 Carlton House Terrace, London SW1.

The Society of Limners, 2 Glentrammon Close, Green Street Green, Orpington, Kent BR6 6DL.

Society of Miniaturists, 41 Lister Street, Riverside Gardens, Ilkley.

The following Societies exhibit in the Westminster Gallery, Central Hall, Storey's Gate, London SW1: Society of Botanical Artists (March), Society of Women Artists (May/June), Society of Miniature Painters, Sculptors and Gravers (November).

The Ulster Society of Miniaturists, Bangor, Co. Down, N. Ireland, BT19 1BX.

Societies in the United States

Arizona: Husberg Fine Art Gallery, 7133 E. Stetson Drive, Suite 1, Scottsdale, AZ 85251

Joy Tash Gallery, 7236 E. First Ave, Scottsdale, AZ 85351

Settlers West Gallery, 6420 N. Campbell Ave, Tucson, AZ 85718

California: G.W.S. Galleries, 256390, Carmel Rancho Lane, Carmel, CA 93923

Colorado: Aspen Art Museum, 590 N. Mill St, Aspen CO 80904 Tel: 303/634-4075

Connecticut: Greenwich Workshop Galleries (GSW), 2000 Post Road, Southport CT 06490 Tel: 800/243-43260

Florida: Miniature Art Society of Florida, President (1987) Mrs Sarah Heyward, 1871 N. Washington Ave., Clearwater, FL 34615

Georgia: Georgia Miniature Art Society, President (1987) Mrs Irene Kemp, 475 Mayes Road, Powder Springs, GA30073 Tel: 404/422-2930

Minnesota: Write Mr W. Grewe, Route 1, Box 24, Gibbon, MN 55335 Tel: 507/834-6335

Wild Wings Gallery, S. Highway 61, Lake City, MN 55041 Tel: 612/345-5355

Montana: Montana Miniature Art Society, Pegee Haman, 3030 Stinson, Billings, MT 59102 Tel: 406/656-1167

Artists' Union Gallery, 31 S. Willson Ave., Bozeman, MT 59715 Tel: 406/586-3636

La Petite Gallerie, 23 West Main, Bozeman, MT 59715

New Jersey: Miniature Art Society of New Jersey, 1591 Broad St, Bloomfield, NJ 07003 Tel: 201/338-0026

New Mexico: Gallery La Luz, Box 159, La Luz, NM 88337 Tel: 505/437-9524

Oklahoma: Gilcrease Institute, 1400 Gilcrease Museum Rd, Tulsa, OK 74127 Tel: 918/583-3122

Texas: Altermann Art Gallery, 2504 Cedar Springs Rd, Dallas, TX 75201 Tel: 214/871-3035

Collectors Covey, 15 Highland Park Village, Dallas, TX 75205 Tel: 214/521-7880

Musselman River Walk Gallery, 123 Losoya Ave, B-19 San Antonio, TX 78205 Tel: 512/226-2255

Washington DC: Washington Society of Miniature Painters, Sculptors and Gravers. President (1987) Mrs Margaret Hicks, 1607 Crittenden St NW, Washington, DC 20011 Tel: 202/291-6404

Wyoming: Laramie Art Guild, PO Box 583, Laramie, WY 82070 Tel: 307/745-5047

Trailside Galleries, PO Drawer 1149, Jackson, WY 83001 Tel: 307/733-3186

Canada

Toronto: Del Bello Gallery, 363 Queen Street West, Toronto, Ontario M5V 2A4 Tel: 416/593-0884

Suppliers of Materials for Miniature Painting

Most good Art shops supply the various types of Bristol board or Arches paper HP, Ivorex, card, Artists' Quality watercolours, gouache or oils, a reasonable quantity of sable miniature painting brushes, with sizes from 00000 to 4; or they will order them.

Other materials, such as ivorine, vellum and an excellent stock of artists' materials are available from:

L. Cornelissen & Son, 105 Great Russell Street, London WC1 3RY or Tel: 071-636 1046.

Frames

Many framers will make miniature frames from left-over pieces of mouldings, quite inexpensively, and provide mounts. Or frame the miniatures to order.

Mail Order Specialists

Polymers Plus, PO Box 101, Christchurch, Dorset BH23 7ES Tel: 0202 470783. Frames, ivorine, mounts, brushes, etc.

R.S. Frames, 4 Broomfield, Sunbury-on-Thames, Middlesex TW16 6SW Tel: 0932 783320. Supplies of metal and wood miniature frames, brushes, ivorine, vellum etc.

R.J.W. Products, 1 Georgian Close, Hayes, Bromley, Kent BR1 7RA. For ivory, ivorine, vellum, brushes and frames for the miniaturist. (Not square or rectangular in wood.)

Framecraft Miniatures Ltd, 148-150 High Street, Aston, Birmingham B6 4US. Frames of all sizes for the miniaturist including brooches and pendants and some wooden oval ones.

The Author

Jo Clay has had several professions. First, studying Engineering before the war led to her working for the BBC on the technical side for two years; but as women were denied promotion at that time, she left for a nurse's training at St Bartholomew's Hospital during the War. After marrying a Bart's doctor and living for ten years in Canada (where she studied Art and Sculpture), she obtained a degree in Italian and English and took her Teacher Training at the University of British Columbia. She was widowed in 1966 and returned to Britain with her four children to teach English in a grammar school. She remarried in 1971 and moved into Adult Education, where she taught Creative Writing in various Colleges of Education or Arts Associations. She and her husband came to live in Dorset in 1988. By then she had been painting miniatures for about five years and has had work accepted at the RMS. Now she has a class in Sherborne and has founded the Sherborne Miniature Painting Society.

Several of Jo Clay's students have had work accepted at the Hilliard Society and the RMS. This book evolved since she believes Miniature Painting should be more widely appreciated. Because of that she has written several features for the *Leisure Painter* about miniatures. She writes mainly about Art, but this is her first book. She hopes there will be others. Her husband Anthony, on retirement, took up wood turning, but is now much involved with making mosaics. They have a very artistic household, which they hope will influence their many grandchildren. As will be obvious, she believes in the personal value of the constructive use of leisure.